Both Sides Of The Curtain...

Geneviève Ward, Richard Whiteing

BOTH SIDES OF THE CURTAIN

From the Painting by Hugh G. Riviere.

Yours sincerely,
Genevieve Ward

BOTH SIDES OF THE CURTAIN

BY

GENEVIÈVE WARD

AND

RICHARD WHITEING

*With a Colour Frontispiece
and Sixteen Other Plates*

CASSELL AND COMPANY, LTD
London, New York, Toronto and Melbourne
1918

CONTENTS

LIST OF PLATES

BOTH SIDES OF THE CURTAIN

CHAPTER I

THE DOYENNE OF THE STAGE

THE great professions, especially Literature, Art and the Stage, delight to honour their senior members—the Stage most of all. This is more to my present purpose, as the Stage admits of a *doyenne*. At this moment its place of honour is held by an American, Miss Geneviève Ward.

Towards the end of March, year by year, and in London where she lives, she has what may be described as a virulent attack of birthday. Her faithful Press trumpets the news of the seizure. The morning mail brings its interviews, its sheaves of letters, and its bouquets by command or otherwise, from both hemispheres. The caller calls—usually to assure her that in her honour Time has performed his favourite " trick act " of running back, and that she looks younger than ever. This was the even course of the ritual of 1916, when she entered her eightieth year; and the completion of the term was duly celebrated in the same way in 1917.

As almost her oldest living friend in years, as in the period of our intimacy, I took care on the

B

former occasion to be the first to arrive at her villa in the neighbourhood of Regent's Park.

This gave her plenty of time to await the others, and I was invited to join her in her morning walk.

"Why not a turn round the garden," I said, "with its promise of spring? It will serve to remind me of your old Quaker city of Philadelphia, or, better still in the circumstances, of some scene out of a well-mounted play. That cosy little church closing the view from the drawing-room may come in so handy for the fourth act. Besides, I have had my walk on the way here."

"I don't call that exercise; it's philandering— and at our age! I wouldn't ask you, but my maids are busy this morning."

"What have they to do with it?"

"I take them with me by turns; I hate walking alone."

"But why?" I protested, as we crossed the canal bridge into Regent's Park.

"Each is my Molière's housekeeper! I make a point of letting her see all the new pieces, and in return get many a new point in the course of our rambles."

"A sort of supplement to the Gallery Club?"

"And a better one, as being a club without a snarl to live up to. She goes to the play just for one thing, to have a good time. Not a theory in her pocket—only to be made to laugh, cry, or get into a rage with the villain, and to nibble a chocolate for her recovery between the acts."

The Doyenne of the Stage

We were making the circuit of one of those dwarf lakes that are to be found in every self-respecting park, a thing which a giant of the prime might have covered with his palm, yet with suggestions of infinitude in every cunning curve.

I mused.

"Out of breath?" she laughed.

"Something much more serious, I assure you."

I was thinking of her extraordinary career in many fields of art, sometimes only with the prentice hand, as in painting and sculpture, at others in full achievement, as in opera and drama. Her whole education, by the luck of circumstance, the best of all preparations for life. Transferred at six years of age from New York, where she was born, to Texas, an excellent substitute for the riding school, and where the horse to mount was also a horse to conquer from the start. Her father's cousin, Colonel George Ward, a venerable survival of the regular army and the Texan war, was her mentor here, with "up you get and on you go" for his simple plan. She learned to gallop before she knew how to fall off. Her father was in business—what self-respecting father of that time was not? Her mother set her the good example of living to eighty-four, and took all the children betimes to Europe to see the world. It was topography, manners, customs—all without tears, and, incidentally, with song as a plaything before it was an art. She saw France and Italy at a very early age, prattled in their idioms as to the manner born, and picked up Spanish without going to the country. Her good angel, she

3

says, spared her Germany. England came later on. But there came a time when the mother had to insist on her settling down to one thing, and more or less to one place, for a career as well as for a living; and music in Italy was her choice.

The omens were favourable. She was built for opera in face and form, fine expressive features of the brunette cast, eyes of particular brilliancy, and a figure that was just so between short and tall. Her voice was another asset, a soprano, but with the register of three in voice control that included the mezzo, and enabled her to sing in parts of varied range. This was in a manner unfortunate, as being rather too much of a good thing, since it tempted her to achievements which in the end strained the vocal cords. However, it was so promising that Rossini consented to guide her studies. It was hard work, of course, with its incidents of dramatic effect that were not exactly in the curriculum. Once, in mid-winter, on the summit of the Col di Tenda, and in a hurry to get through from Turin to Nice, her mother and herself were stopped by the snow. The diligence had given it up as a bad job. The local postmaster offered them mules that might be trusted to slide or hobble down the pass. They were accordingly strapped on, feet facing the sky, and it was done. A far from amiable-looking wolf in attendance gave needless zest to the adventure by incessantly baying news to the pack.

She made a first appearance in *Lucrezia* at Milan, but that was only to get rid of the stage fright; and the real début came afterwards in Bergamo. Then it was Paris, at the Italiens, in *Don Giovanni*, with Mario, Frezzolini and Persiani; Bucharest; London, in English opera at Covent Garden as Maid Marian in Macfarren's *Robin Hood*; Elvira in the *Puritani* at Her Majesty's—all as incidents of a six years' operatic career, closing with New York and Cuba.

There would have been much more to recall, but by this time we had reached her gate.

"Gyp! Gyp! Gyp! That dog! Oh, there he is. Have I scared you? What *did* you think I was crying over the housetops?"

"A sort of coronach, perhaps, for the failure of your voice in Cuba. One of the sharpest of your trials till you turned it into a triumph by seeing it through. All know you as a star of the stage: few remember you as a star of opera. In each case you bridge two epochs of an art: the old Italian school of music and the double Dutch one of to-day—the drama from the French and the classic revival of the Shakespearean school."

"Oh, that is very ancient history now; and, you see, all the dog's history is still to write. I wouldn't lose him for the world. Such a dance, though, sometimes. Besides, he is one of us: he has been on the stage, and not even as a mere walking gentleman, for I carried him in my arms. He's simply the dearest—but never mind. You won't come in? Well, be sure you come to luncheon to-morrow. I want you to try a new *risotto*—perfection!"

Both Sides of the Curtain

"Where's the use of going to luncheon with you? You set such a bad example. Brillat-Savarin himself couldn't have been a more exasperating host."

"And what was his offence, pray?"

"A meal fit for a banquet in Olympus, and for his share of it a morsel of bread dipped in a spoonful of gravy. You may not be aware of it, but such Spartan severity is not exactly an appetiser for your friends. It makes them feel they are eating to satisfy the wants of nature, which is gross. Many a second helping have I forgone on this chilling consideration—'what must she be thinking of me now?'"

"That she hopes you are having a good time. Woman, you know, is—or was, for the fashions change so—by nature a ministrant being. It flatters her to think she is indispensable to the happiness of others. I did not cast her for the part or she would have had a stronger one. It was you, I think, who first called my attention to my favourite text: 'Set on the great pot, and seethe the pottage for the sons of the prophets.' A very woman-hater might hold her harmless in that capacity, though some, I'm afraid, think the only way of finding a use for her is to have her made up in tabloids. Poor fellows! gormandising is about their only chance in the deadly sins. *Au revoir!* Remember, half-past one. Don't come in the morning: I shall be going for my exercises to Sandow."

The voice in opera had failed gradually, not

6

exactly with a snap. It had been worn out with the fatigues of the tremendous repertory. At this period, too, the father had fallen upon evil times with some of his speculations: so, the family luck having given out, she had at once to set about making a fresh supply of it on her own behalf. The mischance, of course, betokened the ruin of one part at least of a career, and many would have taken it as decisive in regard to all hope of public distinction. But she was made of stouter stuff; and she had known, as we shall presently see, an even greater sorrow and a greater trial, and conquered it by her indomitable will. There was still the stage, as another way. But, as elsewhere Miss Ellen Terry has told us, at this period there was no living American drama as there is now; and Shakespeare in adequate production, or even romantic plays in a setting on the grand scale, were still unknown in the States. On the other hand, her speaking voice was still a perfect instrument, capable of all the modulations of passion and feeling; and her wide familiarity with the masterpieces of dramatic literature gave her some assurance on that point. But hitherto she had read only for delight, and she had now to face the colossal task of the creation of another repertory. So she settled down in New York as a teacher of singing, while, incidentally, keeping house for her father. It was done by working out a Daylight Saving Bill on her own account, rising at six and keeping it up till midnight. In this way she contrived to master fourteen parts in drama, among them Lady Macbeth, Beatrice,

Both Sides of the Curtain

Hermione, Portia, and Queen Katharine, with Adrien Lecouvreur, and the Lucrèce, for Lucrezia, of Hugo's play.

This, while biding her time for an opening, generally the last and worst impediment of that curious obstacle course, a public career. England was hardly more encouraging in the outlook than America, but she crossed the ocean for a nearer view. It was still far from inviting. London was all for Gaiety burlesque, Old Drury was fumbling with all sorts of unholy ventures in the line of "may our endeavours to please be crowned with success." Sala, soundest of counsellors when he was not his own client, was taken into consultation; and his suggestion was to try one of the great provincial theatres—at Manchester by preference—for a bit of serious work: "You will get your hearing there, and if you succeed you will have London on the rebound." So, in due season, the Manchester Theatre Royal announced the début of Miss Geneviève Ward in Lady Macbeth, and the all-powerful *Guardian* of next day chronicled the perfect success of the experiment. This was in 1878, and it marked another turning point by giving the new career a triumphant start which was made good in all that followed. Subsequent performances in England and in America were but stages of a final tour round the world. But the full story of these great ventures and of the dignified leisure of her retirement in the plenitude of her powers, without one farewell performance—still less of a series—is not for this place.

8

AN EARLY PORTRAIT OF MISS GENEVIÈVE WARD.

From a Painting.

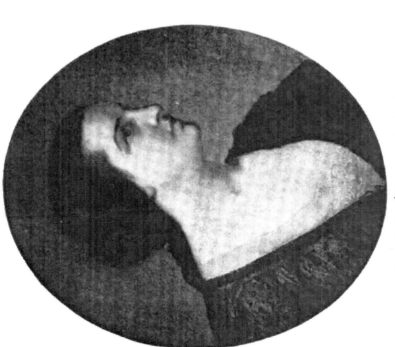

MISS GENEVIÈVE WARD AT 22.

From a Painting by May.

The Doyenne of the Stage

For all that, the life of the player in retirement is a trying thing. The greater the triumphs the heavier the miss of them when all is done; nothing to compare with it in the sharpness of the contrast between past and present. Applause for your daily breath, as well as for your daily bread, and that "hot and hot" as payment on delivery. Here and now is the word: you can hardly afford to give credit till to-morrow's notice. It positively unsexes the meaner sort of men like shipwreck or the cry of "Fire!" and makes them ready to hack their way to it through the scrum over the bodies of their mates, petticoated or not. To all others—the statesman, soldier, man of affairs—glory comes with a more halting pace. The soldier's mention in dispatches has yet to be—to say nothing of his monument. The statesman's reward is a mere undated draft on history. The poor business man has never had and never looked for anything of the kind. But for the actor every night and every minute of the night is his triumph or his despair. Coolness in the house, the moment it has passed the footlights, is chill to the bone. Add to this the intense excitations of the whole medium in which he moves —mighty passions, great actions, the glitter of pageantry, the whole personality wrought up to the achievement of the highest in human conception. The proudest monarch in the world knows nothing to match it in realities or in dreams. Think of all this for a farewell performance that keeps the promise of its title, and then of the too immediate drop to "the rest is silence" of the night that

9

follows, with all the others in its train, cheered by nothing more exciting than an evening party, or in actual practice often only a quiet rubber, or even a "patience," and so to bed. In the midst of all this maybe the pitiless clock tells you that the brilliant house is filling with celebrities for a début of somebody else, that the orchestra is in full blast, and the sudden hush that heralds the rise of the curtain marks the expectation of a new heirship to these intoxicating joys. "Macbeth does murder sleep," indeed, when the part is in the hands of the other man. No wonder my good friend must still be doing something, if it is only knitting stockings for the soldiers, or, in spite of all her vows to the contrary, occasionally allowing herself to be wheedled into the acceptance of another engagement—just to quicken the pulse. What funny scenes of this sort I have seen in her own drawing-room, manager and even manager's wife plying her with delicate flatteries, as the sole Arabian bird of omen for the success of the piece.

The date of the Manchester performance is of import in another way. It marked the disappearance from the bills, as it had long disappeared from private use, of the Madame Guerrabella of opera, and the resumption of her maiden name of Geneviève Ward.

Yet she was Madame Guerrabella after all, though in strict right she was entitled to sign Countess Constantine de Guerbel, by virtue of her early marriage with a Russian nobleman. The story has to be told if only because it has been told so often and nearly always wrongly. Its embellishments add nothing to the poignancy of its interest : the plain unvarnished tale best suits the nature of the subject and the self-respect of the principal character. She was still in her teens and in the plenitude of her grace and charm, when she accepted an offer of marriage from de Guerbel, a member of an old Swiss family which had migrated to Russia in the time of Peter the Great. This, in its nature, if not altogether in its results, was a tragedy which reduces the subsequent disaster of the failure of the voice to the proportions of melodrama. She may well say, when she cares to say anything about it, that the greatest drama of her life has been one in which she never played. It had the strongest situations, the most momentous decisions, at very short notice indeed, and the most thrilling curtains act by act, and yet no audiences, and no limelight. At the time of her first meeting with de Guerbel she was travelling with her mother in southern Italy, and he gave out that he was carrying dispatches for the Tsar. Then, and subsequently at Nice, where there was nothing against his name, he became what Victorian chaperons used to call exceedingly attentive to both mother and daughter, and eventually made his offer of marriage in due form.

The offer was accepted. There was then no Russo-Greek church either in Nice or Turin, so the pair were married by civil contract at the American Consulate. This was on the understanding that the daughter should return to her mother's home until all the parties could set out for Paris together for the completion of the ceremony in the Russian church. It was based on the ordinary practice in many countries in which civil marriage is in use. Where such a marriage is the only one recognised by law, as in France to this day, Roman Catholics regard it as merely a kind of betrothal, and the pair, though already man and wife according to the code, separate at the door of the Mayoralty to meet again for the church ceremony the next day. In this instance it was first arranged that all the parties should travel to Paris by land, but de Guerbel, on the plea that Geneviève was already his wife, tried to persuade her to make the journey with him, leaving her relatives to follow by another route which he knew they preferred. The mother objected, and she had her way. The daughter remained in her care, and, though de Guerbel reached Paris in due course, he contrived, on all sorts of frivolous excuses, to defer his appearance at the Russian church, and finally left for the south.

Months passed without news of him, until it was discovered that he was making arrangements for his marriage with a Russian heiress, a daughter of the Russian Ambassador at Naples.

Mother and daughter at once set out, in the depth of winter, to lay the whole matter before the Tsar. It was a trying journey: from Königsberg to Riga they travelled by sledge, changing every two hours in the snow.

At Petersburg they stayed with the American Minister, Governor Seymour, a distant relative of the Wards, and had his help in drafting a petition to the Autocrat. The matter had now got wind. General Gabriel de Guerbel, elder brother of Constantine and head of the family, called on the Minister for particulars, and was constrained to plead for some compromise that might save what he was pleased to call the honour of his name. The Wards were inexorable on this point: they had been angered to exasperation by his brother's attempt to treat even the civil marriage as an entire fabrication. Meanwhile they had nothing to do but wait; the girl quietly keeping up her heart— and her music, and on one occasion appearing at a reception leaning on the arm of her husband's brother, who had chivalrously left the honour of the name to take care of itself.

One day, at length, their host had a visit from Count Adlerberg, a man high in the confidence of the Court. The diplomatist guessed his friend's errand in a moment: it was a prudent operation in " soundings " on the question of the hour. He accordingly led Madame Constantine de Guerbel into the room, and left the pair together. The courtier was urbanity itself. He gave a patient hearing to the whole story, while carefully holding his peace on the merits of the case, and withdrew, " after compliments " worthy of a complete letter-writer in Chinese. He was speedily followed by an aide-de-camp from the Palace who, without further beating about the bush, wished to know when the daughter of Mrs. Ward could receive Prince Dolgouriki, a member of one of the great historic families of Russia, and high in the confidence of the Autocrat. There could be but one answer—as soon as he liked. The Prince came, was extremely amiable, and went away in full possession of the thrice-told tale, and with the generous and altogether hopeful admission: "He's not good for much, I'm afraid." Caution still prevailed when he came once more and stood on the threshold: "But what is it you want the Tsar to do?"

The lady was ready with her answer: "To have my marriage sanctioned by the Russian Church."

"I will tell His Majesty exactly what you say," was his parting word.

Meantime the sad hero of the adventure had been wandering about the Continent, while still giving his country a wide berth. He was at last overtaken by an Imperial order to report himself at Warsaw for the religious ceremony. Mother and daughter had been already told to await him there; and they were looking for news when they received a telegram announcing his arrival, requesting an interview, and rashly signed as from "your affectionate husband." It came in time to be shown to Mr. Ward, who had now "joined" in this crisis of the family affairs. It is needless to say that it completely gave away the writer's case, since he had hitherto denied the fact of the marriage in any form.

The meeting took place at first between the parents and the sorry bridegroom, and then between him and the bride. It ended on both occasions in nothing but idle protestations of his readi-

ness for the ceremony and of his hopes of a happy
life ever after on his estates in Little Russia—
vaguely understood, on their part, to be somewhere
out of the world. It would probably have been
more consonant with the wife's feelings if the conversation could have been confined to observations
about the weather. The thing rankling in her heart
was that he had not only deceived her, but dragged
her in the mire by persistently alluding to her as
"Miss Ward"; "Hell hath no fury like a woman
scorned."

The gruesome bridal took place next day in the
cathedral at Warsaw. At eleven o'clock the lady,
in black from head to foot, and her party entered
the crowded church. The bridegroom was at hand;
the Archbishop officiated by command. The con-
tracting parties held lighted candles, one of which
—not that of the bride—was observed to gutter
without the aid of a breeze. When it was all over
the Archbishop offered his congratulations to the
happy pair! The bride thanked him in a low voice,
bowed to her husband, leaving him where he stood,
took her father's arm, and, with her party, made
for their carriage and drove away. Another carriage, packed with their luggage, stood ready in the
courtyard of their hotel. In a few minutes they
were at the railway station; in a few more, on their
way to the frontier.

All had been foreseen, including the possibility
that the lady's master, under Russian law, might
collect his wits sufficiently to claim the custody of
her person. The travellers carried a special pass-

port permitting them to leave the country at their pleasure.

They never met again. He subsequently followed her to France and ransacked her apartments, only to be warned that he would be deported on a repetition of the annoyance. Years after, when in New York, she heard of his death at the close of a sordid career.

She never sought for a divorce, as she had once thought of doing, for she had no desire to marry again. She made no claim to his estates. All that she took at his hands was all she wanted—the right to bear his name. This was subsequently modified into Guerrabella on her appearance in opera, and finally dropped altogether when she went upon the stage.

A plain tale is the best, and here it is, on authority. Most of the others belong to the region of fancy. One of them exhibits the heroine at the feet of Alexander II., and sobbing forth her woes. As a matter of fact she never sought speech of him. No doubt she had one powerful friend at court in the person of the American Minister. These were still the days of Russian hopes of an American Alliance against Europe—to avenge the Crimea.

It was a battle won for the whole sex. The marriage laws of the world, in their cruel perplexity, are still the scandal of the time. To take but one instance, thousands of English-speaking women are married by their own national rite in foreign countries, only to find, when it suits their partners to cast them off, that they are no wives at all. The foreign rite has naturally its claims in the foreign land, and where this has been omitted, in all or in one of its innumerable formalities, the woman is at the mercy of the man. Most women so betrayed wear out their lives in silent sorrow or in futile personal protest and personal appeal. Geneviève Ward was of another stamp.

I now leave her to speak for herself, mainly throughout the book.

R. W.

CHAPTER II

EARLY TRAVEL AND SONG

MY first voyage to Italy, where in after time I was to learn to sing, was made in 1840, when I was in my fourth year. We embarked on a wooden sailing ship, even at that period wholly devoid of a sense of the ridiculous as a mode of travel.

My mother kept a log of the voyage: she was thorough in everything; and a mere diary would have been beneath her notice. Here it is now, in my hands, and in yellow ink that only once was black. It is ruled in columns, with the most mysterious headings—"H.K.F. Courses—Winds—Leeway—Air," and so on, and it affords evidence of a valiant attempt on her part to do justice to them in a seamanlike way. When this fails she takes a mean advantage under "Occurrences," to get in something about the baby and the two other children under her wing.

The entries begin with "3rd day of November, 1840." On this day: "The barque *Marcelle*, from New York towards Genoa," casts off from the wharf at 10 A.M. What an abyss of time between! The Victorian era still in its infancy, to say nothing of the mid-Victorian, only a thing of prophecy and

Early Travel and Song

hope! And what a voyage!—an almost solid seven weeks of fair and foul, before we come to anchor inside the " new mole " at Genoa, on the 21st December. It was still, perhaps, a fair record of rapid travel in that remote age.

At the outset we are favoured with a short explanation for the benefit of the landlubber: " A nautical day commences at 12 at noon, and ends next day at 12." It is the last he will get, and for the rest he has to shift for himself. " Variation ¾ Pts. Sandy Hook, bearing by compass West by South, distant 6 miles. Took in top gallant sails at 1 A.M. and double reefed the top sails at 1½." The rather unworkmanlike " All of us sea-sick " ends the somewhat hurried account for next day. Worse is to follow on the morrow. At one moment we are " only 10 miles from the Capes—and in shoal water." But the discreet captain, though " he thought we would be lost," never breathed a word of it till they were safely anchored at Genoa. " Children only just commencing to eat," the day after that, and then but in half rations, for " The goat which I took for baby's milk is sick also and gives none." Poor baby, and, in a way, poorer goat! She dies a few days later—worse and worse! Children on deck about this time: " Lee "—my elder brother—" frightened at first, but Jenny liked it."

Tuesday, a week out, " Baby doleful at sea when it rains, but Providence is over us: He that holds the winds in the hollow of His hand will save us." Ninth day: " Baby sick again; the rolling of the sea is horrible." Tenth day: " We find our apples delicious." Well, well, how many of us have not disdained the same confession on the ocean grey-hounds of to-day! "How terrible the thunder sounds at sea; nothing to break its strength; and the lightning as though the heavens opened." Quite so. Eleventh day: "Severe storm: and to be alone on the wide ocean with no one to speak to, not knowing what next moment will bring forth! Children and nurse asleep; I alone to keep watch. Capt. on deck." A little later that weather again and pumps busy. "What a shock it gave me when that jolly boat broke. Awful! Awful! Baby has a sore mouth and we have nothing to relieve him except some gum arabic. God keep him!" Full calendar month: all hardships forgotten, and quite an old salt now. "Set the top-gal-sails and spanker; at 11.80 set the gaff top sail." Then, in due course: "Cadiz lighthouse, distance 15 miles. Oh, what joy in the sight of land! Passed Gibraltar Rock, dist. 5 miles."

Genoa, and landed at last! But quarantined too—still, perhaps, gratefully, because we can now afford to throw our sea legs away.

I returned to America before I was six, and we went for a year to Texas, returning to France and Italy when I was eight. Then it was that I was in Rome when Pius IX. was enthroned. We returned to America in 1848, thus escaping the *coup d'état* in Paris. In 1858, when I was sixteen, we returned to Florence to begin my studies for opera.

Opera was a very simple affair at that day. Rossini, Donizetti, Bellini, Verdi, Meyerbeer were the chief composers: music was a delight to the ear, not a problem in mathematics. Surely there was enough to learn under the old system. Declamation was finding its way into the programme when I began; and I was sent to Uberti, a poet, and a man as mild as a dove, when he had not to remember that he was the reddest of Red Republicans. He used to prepare little pieces for my benefit—idylls he called them. First he read them to me for look and gesture; then I had to return the compliment to him with any additions I thought proper to make out of my own head. One of these scenes was about the corsair and his bride, who, at that time, had the ballad pretty well all to themselves. The corsair goes out to business in the usual way, but returns minus his boat, and indeed his life. The waves cast him at the lady's feet! Problem: utter the cry proper to the situation. I could not manage it for some time, and at last Uberti lost his temper, stamped and glared. I could do nothing now but wring my hands and utter a cry of despair. "The very thing I wanted," he said; and the lesson ended to his entire satisfaction. He taught me the declamatory part of three operas—*Norma*, *Lucia*, and *Semiramide*. Lamperti, far away the best teacher in Milan, was sounded as to taking me in hand for the singing; but when he heard I was an American he expressed doubts as to my mastery of the idiom. I played a trick on him by calling *incognita* as an Italian, to reassure him on that point; and he consented at once. He was a bit of a bear, like most of the others: it was part

of the method. One day, when he was particularly
irritable, he gave me a rap over the knuckles with
a pencil. Castigations of that sort were usually
endured by the pupil with a tear and a promise of
amendment. I straightened myself and looked him
full in the face. He coloured and bowed, and the
incident was closed. He was an old dear all the
same, and not like some bears who make a market
out of a sore head. My experience is that the devil
is not always so black as he's painted—nor the
angel so white.

I have just found a programme of 1857—my
twentieth year—in which my name appears for the
first time as a singer at La Scala, in Milan. My
real début, however, was at Bergamo in Pacini's
Stella di Napoli. This led to an engagement for
Trieste, and I set out for that place, taking Venice
by the way. The Austrians held both cities at that
time. On arriving at Venice we were informed by
an Austrian officer—it was almost martial law there
—that we were to sing in Venice instead of Trieste.
All " society " had flown from Venice ; it looked like
a dead city, yet the German masters were determined
that the inhabitants should put on some sort of a
show of being the happiest people in the world.

I flatly refused, and at once summoned my
brother to a council of war.

" You will have to do it," said my manager.

" Oh, if it comes to that——"

The next morning he called, only to find his
bird had flown. With the help of the hotel keeper,
an Italian, we had been smuggled out to the railway

station in the middle of the night and put into a goods train for Milan. Poor things! They could not get on without their *prima donna*, you see.

The Milanese chuckled over it, and I was a *persona grata* there, you may be sure. There was a Comitato Veneto (Venetian Committee) at Milan, composed of influential Venetian gentlemen, who gave me a diploma of *Citadina Veneta* (Venetian Citizen), of which I was very proud. I soon had an engagement at the Carcano, Milan, and later I sang for the winter season at Bucharest. Then I was ready, on the generous encouragement of Rossini, for the bold step of Paris—where I sang Elvira—and with London to follow.

I studied oratorio in England under Mrs. Groom, the finest oratorio contralto of her day. She was a protégée of Siddons; and, at the close of the course, she handed me a lock of hair which she had cut from the head of the great woman after death. Fanny Stirling took me in hand for *Maritana*. It was hard work, but the merry heart goes all the way; and the way must be long. The younger people of our time try to cut it short, with disastrous results. It is a note of the age. Randolph Churchill's gibe at Gladstone as an old man in a hurry should have been withheld as a warning to himself. Old people must be in a hurry for all they want; but there is really no excuse for the young ones. Some of the wilder spirits now are for knocking it all off within a twelvemonth. Instrumentalists give many years to study—why not singers? for the voice is the finest instrument in the world. As you get on the labour lightens, and each conquest heartens you for the next struggle.

When it is all over, and you come out, you enter a new and delightful world, a world of adventure in a great pursuit. Things happen: even in the old style of incidents on the road from capital to capital. As we steamed along the Danube one day—a joy in itself—on the way from Milan to Bucharest, I noticed five Hungarians in the national costume, and asked the British captain of our boat about them. He told me they were nobles whom he was trying to smuggle out of Austria to join Garibaldi. He feared, however, that the river was too low for his steamer, a large one, to pass the frontier town, in which case he would have to restore them to the stokehole, where they had been hiding, and take them back to Pesth.

"They'll be nabbed as sure as fate," he said, "if the Austrians get wind of it."

My brother Robert was with me, as dispatch agent for the U.S.A., and we laid our heads together.

"Why shouldn't we take them under our wing?" was the idea.

"Do they know English?" I asked the captain.

They were introduced, and I unfolded my little plan: "I am your sick sister, and you are five more brothers."

"Makes rather a family party," urged the real brother. "Clerks at the Consulate, I should say. But have it your own way."

"You must drop your Hungarian and German,"

Early Travel and Song

I said to them, "and learn all the English you'll need between this and the frontier town where we change boats. I'll teach you; let us start at once."

They were soon, with the captain's help, in full fig for their part as English-speaking travellers. One of them had a copy of "Bradshaw" under his arm, the others bore the remaining properties, especially the indispensable sticks and rugs. Meanwhile, I coached them assiduously in their new native tongue, and in their share of the plot.

"If they ask any questions—but perhaps they won't—you 'no understand.' We'll wriggle you through. Americans—such strange, informal people! —see?"

We managed it, with the help of the real brother, who loyally did his best. They safely effected the change from the large steamer to the smaller one, though it was a ticklish few hours while we waited on the latter for the tedious formalities of passports and luggage. But the upshot of it was that we saw them safely landed at Giurgevo, and on their way by diligence to Bucharest, where, of course, they were safe. Their gratitude was something operatic in its effusiveness, but none the worse for that.

Then again, for the fun of it all, the touches of character and manners among your mates of the cast, the Italians especially. Some of these, in my time at any rate, were deplorably ignorant of things in general. They were just singers, bless them! no more.

Both Sides of the Curtain

I was once asked by a soprano why I wore a crown as Semiramis.

" Because she was a queen, you see."

" *Davvero!* Is that so? " was the reply.

To be fair, costume was in the infancy of its exactitude in the 'fifties and 'sixties. We wore crinolines in all parts. You might have caught submarines in them if there had been any about in those happy days. I wore one at the Academy of Music in New York, as Ione, in the opera founded on " The Last Days of Pompeii." I fought against it, but as all my sister singing birds were similarly caged, I had to submit. I was more successful in the struggle against the barbarism when I had to take, in Dublin, the leading part in *The Puritan's Daughter* which Louisa Pyne had taken in London. She had the courage to dress it in white satin, low neck and short sleeves. Think of it only for a Puritan's daughter, of all stage characters in the world. She wanted me to masquerade in the same style. But I insisted on the proper costume—grey merino, high neck, and fichu, and long sleeves. Our *Mayflower* tradition could hardly have been at fault there. She fought the bad fight all the same, and, good, sweet woman that she was, begged me to wear white satin as it was so much more " becoming "! She was short and stout, and, as such, white satin was the greatest of libels on her—on the accepted principle that it told more of the truth.

Other things were very different from what they are to-day, the rehearsals notably. When first I played *Maritana* with the Pyne and Harrison com-

"LA TRAVIATA."

"THE DAUGHTER OF THE
REGIMENT."

"LA FAVORITA."

"BALLO MASCHERA."

IN GRAND OPERA.

pany there was but one rehearsal, and that only with the piano—none with the orchestra. As for the scenery, I had never so much as seen it. I had to go on a voyage of discovery for my entrance until I found a guide in the famous clown Payne, who, while taking no part in the opera, was, I think, drilling the gipsies or something of that sort. Seeing my difficulty, he showed me my way, and suggested my making the entrée in a new and effective manner, in which he coached me on the spot. I accordingly ran on, kneeled, and with one sweeping gesture, enclosed myself in a perfect circle of playing cards, which he had put in my hand. Unbounded applause!

The only mishap I had in my operatic career was in the last act of *Traviata*, and then it was at the expense of somebody else. The part of Alfredo was taken by a tenor whose small stature was by no means in harmony with the proportions of his voice. As he entered in the last act I, as Violetta, had to rise and rush into his arms. I did it with such good will that I toppled him over, and I went a fine fall over his body. Applause once more, which both of us would have been gladly spared.

The jealousy of opera singers—say, perhaps of most performers on the stage—is proverbial. All things considered, how can they help it? In Bucharest, after a duet with the tenor, I was meant, as I afterwards learned, to be the recipient of a magnificent bouquet, thrown by a lady of my acquaintance. My tenor picked it up, and I was about to thank him for his courtesy, when he saved me the trouble by appropriating it on his own account. Applause once more, this time ironical, and I need not say at whose expense. In such matters the house is marvellously quick to understand.

In New York, again, Brignoli, the famous "silver-voiced tenor," with whom I sang in *La Favorita*, gave his "Spirito Gentil" in a way that earned him a well merited ovation. He now withdrew, as required by the action, and I came on as a pilgrim in search of him. I had to sing a few bars, only to learn from my recognition of his voice in a choir behind the scenes, that he had now become a monk, dead to all the world. At this I made a dumb show of despair, and fell prone on the steps of a large cross in the middle of the stage. The audience was deeply moved and "signified the same in the usual manner." The plaudits were still ringing through the house when Brignoli, returning to sing the great final duet, which ends with Leonora's death, quietly appropriated them to himself with a bow. He was soon given to understand, by the chilling silence, that he had made a mistake. But he never forgave me, as the innocent cause of his discomfiture, and would never sing in *Favorita* with me again.

His vanity would have been remarkable in a child. When we sang in Philadelphia the company stayed in the same hotel. One morning he approached two or three of us who were talking in the hall, and taking a pose said : "*Come vi piace?*" (How do you like it?) We had to give it up, for not one of us saw the slightest difference in his appearance. He was disgusted. "Can't you see I've parted my hair on the other side?"

For all that he sang like an angel—make what you will of it! The other part of the question is no business of mine.

And again, the exhilarating stage quarrels, often but a form of exercise.

The Cubans especially are great in this line: it is the old Spanish blood. Their lyric drama is opera within opera, the kernel being the tiffs of the singers with one another, and the public with them. Pit, boxes, and gallery take sides, form parties and cabals, and still, where they are not the worst of enemies, which is rare, are the best of friends. I've heard it is much the same in politics.

It was my fortune to take part in a drama of this kind when we toured in Cuba. The company, as a whole, was a good one, though with parts of least resistance. Adelaide Phillips, an American, our leading contralto, was in particular a splendid singer and actress. I, as the Madame Guerrabella of my operatic career, was engaged as *prima donna di forza* for the stronger parts. There was also a *prima donna leggiera* for the lighter ones, but in consequence of her failure another American lady, the Signora Lorini, by virtue of her marriage with our Italian manager, was summoned from home to take her place.

The change was a mistake in every respect. Her voice was very beautiful, and she was mistress of her art; also she had a pretty face, but her proportions were abnormal, and she could not perform light operas, especially for the Cubans, who wish to enjoy opera as much by the eye as the ear. Therefore, she was given some of my parts, which the public resented (as I was a great favourite) and kept away from the opera house when she sang—I could not, of course, sing every night. The manager then cast me for the page's part in the *Ballo in Maschera*, instead of the part of Adela which was my right and which I had been playing in Matanzas. I, of course, refused the part. They tried to force me to do it by suing me, but my case was so clear that I won on the strength of my contract, poor Signora Lorini singing meanwhile to empty benches. The salaries were not paid, the chorus clamoured for their wages, and finally came to me *en masse* at my hotel and, falling on their knees, implored me to play the page. There was such excitement about it in Havana, they said, that the receipts would be immense and they would get their dues. What could I do? I gave in on condition that I dressed the part my own way (full trunks and high boots, the lace falling over the knees, and a cloak). Well, we played to crammed houses, the choristers were paid, and all went smoothly. Madame Lorini sang some of my parts and I others.

Finally came the night for my benefit—the management announced the *Ballo*. I never knew who started the rumour that La Guerrabella would appear " *sin botas* " (without boots), but the papers took it up, to my great annoyance, and had articles

about my tights having arrived from New York, etc.
I have always believed this was an attempt at revenge by the management.

At any rate, benefit or no benefit, I insisted on
dressing the part as before. I objected to a mere
suit of tights with afterthoughts—all too few. I
was a singer, and I was not going to bring myself
down to that level. The women will understand.
They were pretty boots, though I say it, with a little
cascade of lace work falling over their tops, and just
the things to make the page boy feel that he was the
father of the man. But this would not do for the
manager: he wanted the more showy costume, if
such it was to be called, especially in the fourth act
for the great scene of the ball-room. So, after the
third act, some of his people came to my dressing-
room to insist on the ridiculous "tights." I declined again; and with that the boots became a
casus belli in a trice. The curtain went up on the
fourth act, and there they were once more!

At the sight of them mighty shouts of protest
went up from certain parts of the house, and the
piece was stopped, for the simple reason that it could
not go on in dumb show. To the musically trained
ear there was some compensation in an analysis of
the uproar. All sorts of things were in it, derision,
indignant rage, the whistle, the cat-call—not without apprehension of cats to follow—above all, a distinct cry of "No boots" in the best Castilian left in
the colonies.

I took up the challenge, folded my arms, smiled
at the audience, but shook my head to the conductor

as a sign that I was not going to attempt to utter another note. This, of course, only made matters worse; and it was almost literally the devil to pay, for the rioters seemed neither of this world nor of a better one. Any popular favourite, whether of stage or platform, confronted at short notice with a change of mood, will know exactly what I mean. Here was our tame tiger suddenly "burning bright" with all possibilities of mischief. I knew it might come to the worst at any moment. Time and again your Cuban, with his stored energy of wrath, has wrecked a whole theatre in a few minutes, and sent anything that came to hand—benches, chairs, and not forgetting the inseparable knife—clattering to parterre and stage. Something of the woman there, you will say, provocative and defiant, though feeling she may have to pay for the luxury with her life. All I knew was that I was not going to give in.

It reminds me now of something I once heard from an eye-witness of a street row in a London slum. A fury, in a rage with her bully, was following him with gibes and taunts, till he turned—as no doubt she knew he would—and, with deadly deliberation, forced her to her knees. Then, slowly twisting one hand into her hair, he got her into position to have her face pounded into pulp with the other. All she did was to look up without the faintest trace of resistance or of entreaty. She had had her hour, or her fraction of it; nothing could take that from her; now, of course, he was going to have his. He was stopped in time by a bystander, but there was no hope of anything of that sort in this case. I had friends in the house, but their number made the use of force out of the question. Besides, any attempt of that kind would have given the others just the excuse they wanted for the final rush.

Well, I was now a perfect automaton of settled defiance and disdain. The mere machinery of purpose had simply mastered me; not I—it, in any conscious act. "Oh, what a jolly row it was!" I fancy that was my uppermost thought. They had done me out of my dues, and now they were being done out of theirs. No more opera for me or anybody else until I had my rights. I knew exactly what might happen if—but I was too angry to go beyond that. The sheer terror of the cold steel that masters me in the acted passion of *Forget-me-not* had simply to take care of itself in this real one. The upset had all the reckless bitterness of a first lovers' quarrel, for we had been such good friends up to then. Perhaps we were going to lose one another for ever, for every stage of the dismal business on both sides seemed a nail in the coffin of our romance. I was quite ready to bring them round once more, but not as a suppliant. I think they were in the same mood : each wanted to win and—forgive.

We were at this pass when some decent people began to cry "Shame," and others to applaud in my support, until at length the tumult gradually wore itself out and died down to perfect silence. With this the conductor, seizing the happy moment, waved his baton again; the orchestra obeyed, and it became "as you were" before the beginning of the uproar.

Both Sides of the Curtain

And there was still a climax to come—a favourite Cuban song, not in the part, which I was to give at the end of the performance in honour of the benefit. Their eagerness for that, I dare say, had something to do with their readiness to let me have my own way in the other matter. It was sung to an accompaniment of thirty guitars—three times ten!—in the hands of as many local amateurs of distinction yearning to do or die. With this my new-found friends were so obliging as to lose their heads, or what was left of them, entirely. The song had to be repeated four times. The stage was invaded *en masse* by the stalls; the vanquished yelled delight. How glad I was at last to be carried, rather than led, to my room, where I suffered myself to be unshod at last, but only by my maid.

Thus ended the first and last quarrel I had with my public.

Ask me how I came to think of being so self-willed in it all, and I have only to say, "I don't exactly know." I could no more reason about it than a bulldog could reason about his bite. The Cuban song, as I have said, comes into the reckoning; and, in this respect, their surrender was one more triumph of the principle that like cures like. It was a musical riot appeased by music. The thirty guitars, shall I ever forget them!—throb! throb! sob! sob!—like so many 'cellos in the very anguish of joy. I hear them still across the seas of time, and feel the twitching of the scalp as they conquer a bestial frenzy by a divine.

After my benefit we went back to Matanzas, and

Early Travel and Song

there Adelaide Phillips took hers. This, in one of its results, enabled us to laugh over the whole matter again in caricature. I have to this day a delightful

Une discussion a propos de bottes

From "El Beneficio de Miss Phillips"

brochure of the kind that went the round of the salons. It is called "El Beneficio de Miss Phillips." In one sketch, a giant personage—my father, who was in the house all through—presents me to the management with the fateful boots in strong evidence, as though to signify that I have put my foot down on a resolve. In another, we have a glimpse of Miss Phillips, at home with her brother, whose

From "El Beneficio de Miss Phillips"

highly cultured faculty of doing nothing suggests the *Dolce far niente* of the title. In a third, the lady's adorers make all speed to Matanzas for her benefit, with a disconsolate laggard at the tail of the procession to signify that he has ceased to hope.

FROM DRAWINGS BY GEORGE A. SALA IN
MISS GENEVIÈVE WARD'S ALBUM.

Early Travel and Song

The last exhibits the Signora Lorini in *Norma*,
another of the parts usurped from the Guerrabella
in defiance of the contract. Grasping in one hand
her diminutive husband of the libretto, and of real
life, the very tenor I had the misfortune to topple
over in the *Traviata* in the earlier part of our tour,
in the other their two stage children, the wretched
Adelgisa gives eloquent musical expression to her
regrets over the muddle into which she has brought
the whole family. The point of the jest is that this
tenor, who had the part of the Roman officer, was
anything but a match in proportions with the
priestess, or even with their brace of stage brats.
Her well-known line, " At length thou art in my
hand," is evidently no figurative expression.

CHAPTER III

TWEEDLEDUM AND TWEEDLEDEE

WHEN I was about fifteen, Madame Sontag heard me sing, and she used to tell my mother to bring me to the theatre to see her. She said one of the best lessons I could have would be to watch her. She was a German countess, a very remarkable artist, then in the height of her career. She married and left the stage, but many years after, through misfortune, she was obliged to return to it. She was an extremely pretty woman, and was so young-looking that people might have mistaken her for her own daughter. When she was in New York there was a curious rivalry between her and one of the greatest contraltos, Madame Alboni. They sang at different opera houses, but Alboni elected to appear in the same operas as Madame Sontag. Alboni was an enormously stout woman, with a very beautiful face, and the most glorious contralto voice I have ever heard. It was rather ludicrous to see her, as Amina in *Sonnambula*, walking across the bridge, asleep, with her enormous bulk; nor was this droll effect diminished by the deep voice in the very light music, though it was transposed, of course. But, oh! what a glorious singer she was—one of the

38

greatest. Her rendering of the variations of Rhodes was quite marvellous.

When we went to Florence, a letter from Madame Sontag gave me an introduction to Rossini, who was most kind to me, selected my teacher, and heard me sing once a week. It was a great opportunity for me in other ways, for it introduced me to his "circle." This was most interesting. Every evening he received his friends, many of whom had been his patrons in the musical world, among them the Marquis Zappi and the Marquis Zampieri. The former, an old friend of my mother's, took a great interest in my studies, and was a sort of chaperon for entertainments and balls. The society was highly select in the German way: the Austrians were in power, and a Grand Duke ruled Italy.

Wagner had become known in his own country in the 'forties, though he still had to make the conquest of the world. The Italian school still held its own, and in that I had been reared, with Verdi as the new man. What a mighty struggle it was between them later on—as clearly defined in its issues, and as far-reaching in its own way, as our clash of arms at this hour. It is all very well for the old poet to mock at musical quarrels as nothing but a difference " 'twixt tweedledum and tweedledee"; for those to the manner born the difference reaches down to the very roots of things in the greatest of all the arts. For the Wagnerians, opera was not primarily music, but primarily drama with music for its handmaid, illustrating, in its own august way, a majestic theme of thought and feeling that was the all in all. For the Italians, on the contrary, the libretto was often little more than a gossamer thread of incident to carry a general idea. The melody, in its own incomparable language, did all the rest, and rather disdained co-operation on equal terms. When the air finally knew its business, words seemed very much of a tautology. Plot and character were little more than a framework for embroideries. We had a romantic heroine, always in a sea of troubles, a conventional hero, bound to be in the same case and in the acute stage of disease of the heart, a venerable parent angry and heavy, but not half a bad fellow in the last act, conspirators who gave dark counsels at the top of magnificent voices, a dagger or an equally honest cup of poison for the properties. What matter, so long as the whole thing was lapped and cushioned in the flowing song medium that bore its burden of incongruity like a feather-weight. There were protests, no doubt; and opera, like all the other arts, was no stranger to the process of devouring its own children. A new school, hustling its way to a place, railed at the old one as mere "ear tickling." Donizetti was regarded as a wholesome reaction against the "Bellini syrup," until he in turn had to bear the rude shock of Verdi as the *sans-culotte* of the art, who was to send them all to limbo. Verdi, again, was to feel the Wagnerian lash as a mere "hand-organ man," and so they went on.

It was, in the main, a revival of the controversy, centuries old, between the artist in opera, as a voice and little besides, and the artist in drama, as an

Tweedledum and Tweedledee

exponent of action and character. Both, it was said, should be united in the perfect master of song. So they should, perhaps; so they are and always have been when the Italians have the matter in hand. But the acting must be subordinate to the singing. Italians could not sing without acting: it is natural to them. Mario and Ranconi were finished actors. I, too, was considered so—but, of course, the singing came first.

In my early days certainly, opera was melody, and even when Verdi came upon the horizon he was considered very loud and looked upon somewhat as Wagner is now. His parts strained the voice very much more than Donizetti's, Bellini's or Rossini's; his orchestration was very much louder than theirs, and the artists were obliged to exercise their lungs more. I really don't know what opera is coming to, with the new instruments and methods used now. The voices won't last at all. Mr. Dooley, on coming out of a Strauss concert, gave a description to his friend Hennessy. He said, "When I left the concert I came out into the comparative silence of the elevated railway!" I think that sums it up pretty well. Wagner wears the voice out for his purposes, sacrifices it as ruthlessly as, in another field, his countrymen now sacrifice lives.

All the artists of my time who yielded to this arrogant demand lived to repent of it. Albani was one of its victims, though I hardly like to say so. Such an exquisitely delicate voice, singing in Wagner, was a butterfly harnessed to a steam engine.

41

Both Sides of the Curtain

At the Italian opera in Paris I sang one season with some of the greatest artists in *Don Giovanni* —German, if you like, in its origin, but, as a work by the divine Mozart, wholly in the soul and spirit of the Italian school. Mario was the Don Giovanni, Madame Frezzolini Donna Anna, Adelaide Persiani Zerlina, and I the Donna Elvira. Of course, Mario's part had to be transposed, as it is written for a baritone. He was the perfection of an aristocratic Lothario and quite to the manner born, as he came of good family. Then, that nothing might be wanting, he was extremely handsome, as was his wife, Julia Grisi. I had seen them together in *Norma* when I was eight years old, and I never forgot it. The tympanum was not put to excruciating torture by the braying of brass instruments. The orchestra was an accompaniment to the voice, not the voice to the orchestra. Lablache, the greatest basso of his own or perhaps of any time, was also in the cast. On the stage he made you cower under his spell, but off it he could sometimes trifle with the best; he once made a wager that he could strike more notes at a time than any living pianist, and he won it by sitting down on the keys! They had all made their mark in England. In those days the great objective of singers who came from Italy was, first, Paris for the fame, and then London—for the money, alas! There is this, however, to their credit: they never failed in loyalty to their art, never misused their voices; they did not scream for gold.

Parepa was another fine singer. She had a most

exquisite voice and was a most delightful artist; but, unfortunately for opera, there was a little too much of her, as there was of Alboni. On one occasion, as she preceded Sims Reeves on the platform, in oratorio at Exeter Hall, her massive proportions literally eclipsed him from the view of her audience. "*M. Sims Reeves ne parait pas* (Parepa) *ce soir,*" remarked one wit deliciously, as a sort of double event in puns.

It was not always easy to hear great Italian artists in Italy in my time; they were so soon snapped up abroad. The one I best remember was Giuglini, and for reasons. I was studying in Milan at the time, and he was the favourite at the Scala, where my mother and I usually spent our evenings. One night he was soundly hissed when he appeared. Such an uproar! Cat-calls and everything else objectionable, a discord of abominable sounds. The word had gone round the house that he had stabbed his wife that day at dinner with a table-knife, luckily without killing her. So, when the audience had let him know what they thought of him as a man, they allowed him to get on as a singer—quite as much for their own sakes as for his, for the voice was divine, and they applauded him to the echo. The sharp distinction drawn between the artist and the culprit was quite characteristically Italian, as the nicety of fitting the punishment to the crime was worthy of the most enlightened jurisprudence. It was as though they had adjusted the duration of the cat-calls to the depth of the wound.

This illustrates, rather grimly no doubt, their

attitude towards their favourites of all kinds, and especially towards their singers. These are at once the spoiled children and the masters of the public. They are to be corrected now and then in a fit of ill-humour, but they are still to be petted and admired, and in a way loved.

Mapleson's memoirs abound in instances of this kind. He has told us, almost in terms, that Mongini was a great baby, utterly incapable of reasoning when he was angry, and yet melted into tenderness by a word that appealed to his better feelings. Once, when singing in London, the artist had left a coat with the wardrobe master of the opera to be slightly enlarged. The wretched tailor, in a fit of absence of mind, made it tighter than ever. Mongini demanded either his life or his utter ruin—I forget which. Mapleson faithfully promised that the forfeit should be paid. The next morning the delinquent, duly instructed by the *impresario*, appeared before the singer in a state of utter abasement and informed him that he had been dismissed from the theatre, and that his wife and children—he had neither the one nor the other—were now going forth to starve. Mongini immediately abased himself before the management to beg for the recall of the decree, and when the latter affected to hesitate, offered to sing for nothing for one night, if this were done. The price was not exacted; the tailor was pardoned and the incident was closed.

Giuglini was a creature of just the same emotional sort, not altogether in his right mind at the best of times, and at the worst—well! Later on, when

Tweedledum and Tweedledee

I had taken to the operatic career, he refused to sing with me in the *Puritani*, at Her Majesty's in London, because I resembled the injured wife. It is the condition with most of them, exacted by nature as the price of their extraordinary powers. They live in a world of their own, pure romance on the stage, chilling contact with realities off the stage; and the perfect equilibrium at times and seasons is very hard to maintain.

This is more especially true of the Italians: the Germans, by the nature both of their art and of their minds, are of another stamp. I think that is why theirs are the only voices that can cope with the Wagner orchestration. Their physical capacities are more gross. Yet how great in every way some of them can be. I found that when I sang in *Robert le Diable*, at Her Majesty's, with Titiens, the greatest German artist I ever heard. She was not only a fine singer, but a fine actress. I was comparatively a beginner and she an old-established favourite, yet she was very generous in her association with me.

The German voices have not the exquisite softness of the Italian, and I suppose their training under German masters is of a rougher kind. Their opportunities are certainly fewer nowadays. In Wagner's operas you might almost say there are no songs; it is all recitative, which, of course, so far as the drama is concerned, is more consecutive, but in which the orchestra really usurps the melody—if there is any, though one can hardly discover it. There are a few beautiful things, naturally—the

march in *Lohengrin*, for instance. I have heard it
said that if the master heard anyone humming or
whistling anything from an opera of his he immediately cut it out. I sum it up in this way, that
the Wagner opera is too purely mathematical—I
mean in its time—while the Italian is the reverse.
It is the German *kultur* as opposed to our culture,
two entirely different things with the same name.
Wagner stands for one, and the Italian school for
the other. I have been to concerts where they were
playing some of his outrageous things, and I have
noticed the utterly wearied expression on the faces
of many of the people, as though they were merely
doing what they thought it the thing to do.

We shall come back to the old golden rule
beyond a doubt—think of the singing and the rest
will take care of itself. In the old *Arte del bel
Canto* of Italy they did that as spontaneously and
as naturally as the birds do it now. The singer was
not required to be a preacher, and he left the moral
of his performance entirely to its own devices. The
Germans of to-day affect a perfect contempt for
vocal technique, as it is understood by the melodists
of the Latin nations. The voices have now to play
up, as well as they can, to the loud, blatant music,
and often perish under the process, like recruits
under the drill-sergeant's hand. Madame Marchesi,
perhaps the greatest authority on the subject,
assures us that, if this goes on, the art of singing
is doomed. It would be a pity, for, in and by and
for itself, it is the most beautiful thing in the
world. Patti, who had a keen sense of the value

of her gift, never would sing in Wagnerian opera "in spite of all temptations," as may naturally be supposed. The terrible instrumentalists rule the roost in the Wagnerian scheme. No wonder a German prince, and even a Prussian one at that, described music as " an expensive noise." This contempt for the voice gift is very much a product of the philosophy of the fox in the fable who had lost its tail. Some excellent judges go so far as to say that the Germans never had a voice to lose. Wagner himself, in a moment of unwonted candour, said: "The Germans lack the true methodical voice gift." Beatty Kingston used roundly to declare that the besetting sin of all their operatic artists was sheer singing out of tune. One's "teeth were very punctually set on edge any night of the week" at public performances in Berlin. And this he would make good by a formal indictment by name of a whole list of actor vocalists who seemed to glory in their vice.

The Berlin opera naturally led the way in this campaign of frightfulness against quality, as distinct from mere power. It was the cause of the famous quarrel between Lucca, the queen of Italian song in the Prussian capital, and the ill-trained local stars, led by Madame Mallinger, who could do nothing but shout their way to triumph in the Wagner scores. Mallinger's Nemesis came when she wrecked her voice in the struggle, and had to leave the stage; and Berlin's when Lucca quitted the capital in disgust. The Italians have ever been merciless to all singing out of tune; a false note

may raise a riot in a moment, and from every part
of the house, for the humblest have the ear for the
outrage by a natural gift. What a people they are :
the glory of song! When Verdi, in his eightieth
year, produced his *Otello* at Milan the whole popula-
tion made holiday about it, and a good half of it
were on the verge of delirium. It is noteworthy
that, when I met Meyerbeer in Paris, after I had
finished my studies, he urged me to enter the French
opera and play in some of his works. He said
nothing about going to Germany, for he was always
more French or Italian in the trend of his art. But
my mother wished me to come to her in England,
so that was given up.

In England I met Balfe and his wife, a German
lady. She had a terrible accent for our tongue, and
used always to refer to her husband as " my horse-
pond." I also met Wallace, a charming composer,
and Mrs. Anderson, the pianist to Queen Victoria.
It was through her that I made my *début* in London at the Philharmonic concerts, and I owe her
a debt of gratitude for that. It was a great beginning for a young artist, for the old Philharmonic
never engaged any but classical singers. This soon
led to an engagement for the English opera company at Covent Garden, where I made my *début*
as Maid Marian, in Macfarren's *Robin Hood*, and
sang with Charles Santley. England may be proud
of Santley, the finest and most masterly baritone
I have ever heard. Not only had he as beautiful
a voice as any Italian, but he had his art at his
finger ends. He was also a very good actor, as

anybody who saw him in the *Colleen Bawn* will remember.

It was quite different with Sims Reeves. He, again, was really the voice and nothing besides, the greatest tenor of his day, but a mere stick at acting. I played Meg Merrilies, at Manchester, to his Bertram, in *Guy Mannering*, and he gave "Come into the Garden, Maud" and "You'll Remember Me" in the course of the performance. But the whole thing was absurdly stage-managed. In one of the scenes a couple of ruffians, *à propos* of nothing at all, brought on a stolen piano, dumped it down on the stage, and made off to the cry of, "I hear footsteps—let us disappear." With that, on walked Sims Reeves, and remarking, "Oh, here is a piano; let us have a little music," plunged immediately into one of his ditties, and held you spellbound till he had disappeared in his turn. On this the robbers at once appeared. "Ha, ha! they have gone; let us take her off." And the piano made its exit too. Sims Reeves had no sense of the ludicrous; in the same piece he had the courage to appear in the cave scene in white kid gloves. I never heard him in opera.

Everybody knows what a charming woman Antoinette Sterling was. She was a pupil of Garcia and married Mr. MacKinlay. Her son, Malcolm MacKinlay, is such a successful teacher; he took to teaching singing as his voice failed. Antoinette Sterling's voice was beautiful, but the chief charm of her singing was in the pathos and the sense of humour, which were very keen. Her lighter songs were delightful. Her daughter, my pupil, Jean Sterling MacKinlay, inherits strongly this sense of humour in her acted ballads, with which she has had great success, and she reminds one of her mother. She originated her present charming entertainment of acted songs.

My whole foreign repertory in opera was as follows: *Norma, Lucrezia Borgia, Marta, La Favorita, I Puritani, Roberto il Diavolo, Torquato Tasso, Semiramide, Barbiere di Seviglia, Trovatore, Ernani, Traviata, Ballo in Maschera, Ione, Don Giovanni, Stella di Napoli, Bernabo Visconti, Figlia del Reggimento.* Most of them were Italian from start to finish, and all were most frequently sung in that tongue. A few of the composers were not of Italian origin, and Meyerbeer's *Robert le Diable* was first written in French.

Those sung in English were *Robin Hood, Maritana, The Lily of Killarney,* and *The Puritan's Daughter.*

CHAPTER IV

HOW I BECAME AN ACTRESS

I BECAME an actress because the stage was the sister art of opera, and after a six years' career in the latter I had the misfortune to lose my voice. It weakened through overstrain until I could no longer do what I wanted with it for the lyric stage; and anything less than that was out of the question.

I had been successful; and I may fairly say there was every promise in my past of a career. But what was I now to do? Careers are not taken up or dropped at a moment's notice; each wants its apprenticeship; and—meanwhile? For, with the loss of voice, came other cares in a shortage of means.

Adelaide Phillips, best of comrades, and the greatest American contralto of the time, advised the dramatic stage. I had always tried to be as good an actress as a singer, so I had my path of least resistance clearly at hand. I accordingly went straight to Lester Wallack, in New York, and asked him to try my powers. He gave me a long scene in *Wonder*, a classic of its kind. The rest of the title was *Or, a Woman Keeps a Secret;* but this was gradually dropped, I suppose with the growth of a sense of shame. I was to study it, and come to him again.

I had learned long parts without difficulty in

opera, but when it came to sheer memorising in words, words, words, without music, I was humiliated to find myself rather at fault. Owing to our frequent changes of place in childhood, we never went regularly to school, but were taught at home by governesses and tutors. Recitation had not been included in our studies. The real difficulty, however, was that I did not know how to study a part. Mr. Wallack expected me to act it with him; sheer nervousness overcame me, and I could not face the trial.

In my desperation I went into the country and did my best to coax the singing voice back to its old strength. But the bird was on the bough this time, and would not come down. Only one resource was left; to give lessons in the art of song—a dire drop: it makes such a difference to be fussing about with the others, when all you want is to be busy with yourself. And for that drudgery, at best only the living wage.

So, with hopes still fixed on drama, I set to work in the intervals of the music lessons to get up a repertory for the stage; and in six months I became letter perfect in fourteen parts, and stiff ones at that. It was a bit of a feat, though I say it. I had to seal up all the music cells of my brain and refit with new office furniture of memory, quite another thing. I don't say I learned the plays from start to finish; I do say I learned the particular parts in which I hoped to begin my new career. Here is the list: all Lady Macbeth; all Beatrice in *Much Ado*; Hermione in *The Winter's*

How I Became an Actress

Tale; Portia; Queen Katharine in *Henry VIII.;*
Lucretia Borgia, in English, from Hugo's play;
Bianca in *Fazio,* by Dean Milman; Madame Fon-
tange in *Plot and Passion;* Juliana in *The Honeymoon;* with the leading parts in *Adrienne Lecouvreur; Medea; The Actress of Padua; The
Sheep in Wolf's Clothing;* and *Peg Woffington.*

Fanny Morant was my dramatic teacher, and I
worked with her for everything belonging to the
full and perfect representation—emphasis, gesture,
pose and, above all, for the soul of the part, in
my own reading of it as well as in hers. I rose
early to it, I went to bed late; I gave my singing
lessons; I kept house for myself and my father, the
only one of the family with me at the time. I
began with *Fazio,* and I did actually commit fifty
lines at a sitting. I was told that I should soon
learn two hundred! I hesitated whether to laugh
or cry, but on reconsidering the matter there were
no tears. You see, I was busy, and the laugh took
less time.

And when it was all done America did not want
me.

Miss Morant arranged a hearing for me at
Bryant's Opera House, and rounded up some forty
friends and critics—the terms are by no means
synonymous—to make an audience. They were nice-
ness itself—"pleased to meet you"—flattering pro-
phecies—"good afternoon," and the echoes of the
emptying house.

Try England.

Both Sides of the Curtain

I crossed in 1878. Many remembered me in opera, and that helped to keep me straight for the highest in drama. I was ready to make a compromise for a hearing, but I was firmly resolved that I would only stoop in that way to conquer in the best work. But stars of legitimate drama were not in great demand. Old Drury was going over to the enemy with spectacular pieces. The cry was for showy women with "speaking parts," all afloat through seas of trouble, on rafts of padding with plenty of limelight to show them the way. Even Mr. Bateman, at the Lyceum, could offer but little encouragement, partly, of course, and naturally, because he was so well provided in his own family for the better things.

Then one day a card was brought to me—"The Hon. Lewis Wingfield." I hesitated a moment over the name, but my mother recognised it at once. He was an Englishman who had worked splendidly with her in the ambulance service during the siege of Paris. He had heard of our arrival, and he came to pay his respects and to make my acquaintance.

"I know you by repute already," he said. "Palgrave Simpson has been talking to me about you. I understand you think of trying your fortune on the English stage. Can I be of any use?"

No visit could have been more seasonable: he was a writer, a dramatist, a critic under the pseudonym of Whyte Tighe, and even an actor of some note. He knew all London worth knowing, and withal, as my mother has often told me, and

as it proved, was one of the kindliest and most un-
selfish men in the world. He said :

"All you need, I take it, is a hearing—I want
you to have that on my own account. I think it
ought to be a very simple affair."

He took me to see Mr. Chippendale, "old Mr.
Chippendale" even then, though, I believe, in the
height of his powers as an actor of classic comedy.
Was he ever young, I wonder? I have almost
always heard him spoken of as a veteran. I think
many confused his personal dates of origin with
those of the pieces in which he played. Alas! all
he had to say, though he said it with the charm of
manner proper to his line of study, was that his
company represented the full measure of the ex-
isting demand for work of that kind. It was true;
they had attained a high degree of finish; they
ministered to a select audience of their own; and
that audience just sufficed to them without leaving
room for any new venture of the same sort.

Mr. Wingfield's next attempt was a charming
little breakfast-party at a studio adjoining his house
in Maida Vale—"to meet Miss Ward." A few
critics, a few lovers of the stage, as distinct from
mere patrons. All civilised communities have been
blessed with these, in all the arts and in every age.
It was a breakfast with "speeches" to follow, in
the form of recitations to be given by me. Please
imagine that I was ready to sink into the earth as
the hour of trial approached, and to believe, when
it came, I did nothing of the sort. I gave them
the two or three things which they said were nice

things; and I believe they were sincere. One can usually tell which is which in such utterances, and it cheered me up. It bore precious fruit. After some delay behold me engaged as Lady Macbeth for the great Shakespearean revival at the Theatre Royal, Manchester, in 1878.

That venture was the happy thought of George Augustus Sala. He was a great strategist of time and opportunity, and his counsel was to the effect that my way to London was through Manchester.

"Two favourable lines in *The Guardian* will make you," he said. " Manchester takes the drama as seriously as it takes music; and *The Guardian* is Manchester for wares of that sort."

Kind and constant friend! I had the greatest respect and admiration for him to the last. He took his art of journalism seriously, for no one laboured more assiduously for the instruction by amusement of the million then coming into its own. He made *The Daily Telegraph* and revolutionised the daily paper. On the surface he seemed but the gossamer creature of an hour, touching literature, art, society and manners. But the touch was light only because the hand was sure. He toiled for all his effects, in part because it was laid on him as a sort of primeval curse by his infirmity of semi-blindness. One eye was quite gone for use, but he made the other serve. He read and wrote with his nose to the paper; his script was real calligraphy—beautiful writing. It had the finish of copper-plate. Not this alone : every comma, colon and point was in its place. Nothing was left to the printer's reader : he had but to see and to obey. It was the same with his facts, even when they happened to be but another name for his fancies, as he picked and chose them for the purposes of his art, and art it was. His description of an appetising dish was a perfect recipe for the making of it. Read him on *bouillabaisse à la Marseillaise*, on a French salad, on a Tartar soup *à la Russe*, on the right order and brand of wines. The mouth watered : it was almost a service of grace before meat.

All this went into his part of the agreeable rattle, the man about town, the creature without a thought or a care. He was really a sad and serious being, weighted with bodily ailments and with the gloomiest outlook on life. He had been all sorts of things— scene-painter, journalist, after-dinner speaker, a vocation of itself and carried through just like the rest. Every anecdote was in its place, as carefully edited to the very pauses and inflections and for the terminal words as if he had conned it in triple proof. His drawings exhibited the vice of the method. He did dozens for my albums, but there was no " quality " in them because he never could get away from the particular to the general. If it was costume it looked like something for a fashion plate, as faithful as the photograph in every laboured line. In other things, too, I believe he was at times a little out of his depth. I envy Mr. George Russell the dinner-party at which, as he tells us, he brought Sala and Matthew Arnold together. The talk turned on Virgil, and Sala said he had just been reading— the Georgics, I think—and had come to the conclusion that Virgil was "quite a rough sort of farmer-fellow with leggings and a bill-hook." Arnold was equal to the occasion. "Well, my dear Mr. Sala, somehow I did not think Virgil was quite like that. But your view of him is very interesting." I suppose, by the context, this must have been a terrible heresy.

He was blessed with an old-fashioned wife, the wife ministrant, now quite "gone out," but with his infirmities the very one for him. She had no literature, but she made it her business to help him to realise himself in that way, as he understood it, by smoothing his path. She called at the office of the paper every morning with his proposals for the topic of the day. She bought the pens, ink and paper of his fancy on the way home, and then sat down to take his dictation, if his hand happened to be out of gear. His dictations to her ran somewhat in this way. I take a sentence at random from a scrap of criticism on my work on the lyric stage. "'She (capital S) is an embodiment of the most charming characteristics of literature and art (comma), speaks nearly as many languages as Pico della Mirandola (caps P, M) or Cardinal (capital C) Mezzofanti (capital M, two z's and semicolon); and besides singing (comma) paints (comma) sculpts (comma) and dances with genuine merit (comma) and is the young and beautiful heroine of one of the strangest and most romantic dramas of real life which could be matched anywhere in "Les Mystères (quotation mark, capital L and M, accent grave first e) de la Russie" (quotation ends, full stop).'"

How I Became an Actress

Such are, or may be, the labours that underlie the art of writing a column on a blade of grass—his modest boast. The tribute as to my skill in the tongues is just a trifle overdone. I do not know, though I am sure he did, how many languages there were in the budgets of my illustrious rivals. I am quick at picking them up in the lands of their birth, the only natural and easy way. I really had five to my name, not to count our dear mother tongue —French, Italian, Spanish, German and Russian. German I never liked and have only used when travelling in Germany. Russian I have almost forgotten, not having had occasion to speak it for the last sixty years. But when Sala wrote I spoke the whole batch, with a dialect or two to eke them out in emergencies. I make this humiliating confession lest someone should try me in Hindostanee and put me to shame. Never mind. Bless him, he was always good to me!

Well, the *début* in *Macbeth* came and went; and the next morning in the *Guardian*, instead of the two lines, there were as many as made a column. The writer of the notice was Richard Whiteing. I cherish it to this day, because it was the beginning of a friendship that, on my part, shall certainly never end but with my life. But I give him warning that, if he doesn't pass this in the book we are now writing together, I will never speak to him again. I have told him as much, but all he has to say in reply is that there seems something wrong with the logic. Never mind, again.

Started again, and full steam ahead now. I continued *Macbeth* in Manchester for several weeks, and followed with Constance in *King John*. A *début* in Dublin came in November of the same year, 1873. I played in the English version of Hugo's *Lucrèce Borgia*, and in this, as in the first venture, I began to reap the reward of my previous study of the fourteen parts. I was ready with a whole repertory. In a single fortnight I appeared in *Adrienne Lecouvreur*, *Medea*, *The Actress of Padua*, and *The Honeymoon*. It was an Irish audience, and I won its approval— need I say more? I had the same good luck during a week in Hull that followed, with Portia and with *The Hunchback*, more recently added to my list. At Newcastle-on-Tyne, while playing in *Adrienne Lecouvreur*, my most flattering tribute came from an admirer among the twelvepenny immortals. He was, I regret to say, very much intoxicated, and he insisted on applauding me with a frequency that threatened to bring the performance to a standstill. He was admonished into silence which he seemed to find irksome. For suddenly, clenching his hands in his hair, he roared out : " By —— that woman makes me sober ! "—and, without assistance, left the house.

It was now time for the descent upon London —again thanks to the counsel of the indefatigable Sala. In March, 1874, he gave me an introduction to Mr. Chatterton, then at the Adelphi; and by the end of that month I appeared, under his management, as Unarita in *The Prayer in the Storm*, a melodrama originally called *The Sea of Ice*. It was not the kind of work I wanted to do; indeed, it

was only booked for a fortnight as a stop-gap.
But, of course, I did my best with it, and it stopped
the gap for six months on end. "But one word
of praise," wrote a captious critic, "and this is for
Miss Ward, whose skilful acting saves from utter
condemnation a drama not worth redemption."
Criticism, at least, was beginning to repent of
dramas like *The Prayer in the Storm*, but I do not
repent of my efforts to give the culprit a longer
reprieve.

Chatterton was to be pitied much more than
blamed. He had done wonders for the higher
drama during his long management of Drury Lane,
with the help of such artists as Phelps, Barry
Sullivan, Charles Dillon, Henry Irving and Mrs.
Kendal. He was less than just to them and to
himself in echoing Boucicault's cynical saying that
"Shakespeare spelt ruin and Byron bankruptcy."
Nothing of the sort; as his friend John Coleman
has told us, he fell, not through adventures in great
drama, but in disastrous speculations in other
fields.

So London was won, if not exactly on its merits;
and what was equally delightful to me, America
was coming round. I had all sorts of pleasant
letters from there suggesting a speedy visit. In the
course of the next year's (1875) work in London and
the provinces I played at Drury Lane. Yes, but
not in Shakespeare, only in "the grand spectacular
drama" of *Ivanhoe*. My Rebecca was praised, but
that made me none the happier.

"I called in late at the Arundel," wrote Wingfield, " to hear how it had gone. They (the critics) are by education a phlegmatic set, but said that where you erred was always on the right side. I mean in avoiding clap-trap and rant—which from so cold-blooded a set is no inconsiderable compliment." I pictured them in my mind, still but half warm, and waiting till the small hours till they thawed. The Arundel was the critical club of the time, and its members rarely began to melt till their copy was in the printer's hands and post midnight brought the sense, if not the reality, of sunshine and the opening day.

Ivanhoe was not the *début* of my dreams for Drury Lane. I longed for a prettier dish to set before this batch of Arctic kings, not to be heated into high spirits even by a *Sea of Ice*. Meanwhile, it was London and the provinces for the whole of the year 1875. Wills's *Sappho* at Dublin, and Wingfield's *Despite the World* at Manchester, succeeded *The Hunchback*, *Antigone* and *The Merchant of Venice* (Portia) at the Crystal Palace.

The Crystal Palace performances were under the management of Charles Wyndham, and they gave me excellent opportunities. He was the best of managers, for one reason, perhaps, because he was also the best of artists; he thought only of the piece as a whole, even to the point of absolute self-sacrifice. On one occasion, in *Antigone*, he came on as a supernumerary to fill a void. Such a man commands success, and he had it in full measure. Wingfield, as a dramatist, worked in the same self-denying spirit. His play just mentioned was

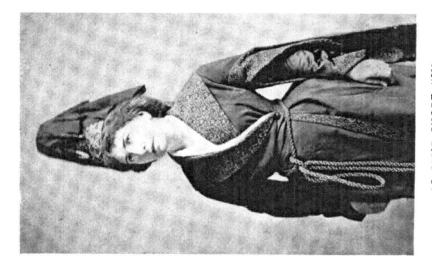

AS JANE SHORE (1876).

AS LADY MACBETH (1876).

founded on an Italian piece, *Cuore ed Arte*, in which Ristori had appeared. She gave me a copy and urged me to have it adapted for my own use. Wingfield took it in hand for me, but, finding the Italian version utterly unmanageable, he turned it into a comedy-drama, which was virtually a new and original work. The setting is the court and period of Frederick the Great, and the leading part of the Countess Thekla fell to my share. "Such plays as this," said one of the notices, "lift the stage above the category of mere amusement, and rank it with institutions of popular education."

At last, in 1876, I was able to make my bow at Drury Lane as Lady Macbeth. I organised the performance for the benefit of the American Centennial Fund, in honour of the hundredth anniversary of the Declaration of Independence.

I had got as far as this when I came to a sudden and yet long-cherished resolve. I decided to stop dead with all new engagements and go back to school again in Paris to study under Regnier, the greatest teacher of the time. So, at the end of 1876 and for some time in 1877, I rehearsed everything rehearsable within my reach with that incomparable master. What pains I took and he took with me! He held all the cards, the tradition and the teaching of Talma, which had given him the views of the more modern school. He carried the fame of the Théâtre Français all over Europe, and was as well known in St. Petersburg as in Paris. A good story served to keep his memory fresh in the Russian capital. He was once arrested there for daring to speak to the Tsar Nicholas in the street without the formality of an audience. As it turned out, the Tsar had first spoken to him by stopping him for a chat. As the autocrat dismissed him with a smile the detectives, whose business it was to dog the footsteps of their unhappy master as if he were the worst malefactor in his dominions, jumped to the conclusion that there had been an unwarrantable intrusion and detained the artist for inquiries. He was soon at liberty again, of course. But when, a day or two later, the Tsar, who had known nothing of the issue of the first encounter, beckoned him again for another gossip he boldly declined : " Please do not address me, Sire ; your Majesty's conversation is compromising." Then the whole story came out : the ruler of millions had his laugh, the player his vogue for the joke.

The teaching for the French stage is the most thorough thing of its kind in the world. I studied privately under Regnier ; beginners go first to the school of the Conservatoire, where many of the greatest actors of the Français take the classes in turn for a fee that does little more than cover the cost of their cab fares. No single thing is omitted —gesture, declamation, the search for the author's innermost meaning ; above all, the sense of the absolute unity of the performance in the due subordination of the part to the whole. No one must try to score simply and solely for himself. No nicety of the grammar of the art is beneath the notice of the master. I have before me at this moment a tiny treatise in a nutshell that M.

How I Became an Actress

Boissière, President of the Société Philotechnique, placed in my hands on "those elements of pronunciation which ought to be known to all persons of our nation." It is written on a strip of paper, some two inches by four, yet well dissects the principal letter sounds of the language. Beginning with the vowels we have three sounds for *a*, four for *e*, winding up with eight "strong sounds" of the consonants, eight "weak" ones, and four more to complete the count. This, of course, was only the groundwork; for the finished result of that and ever so much more one had to see the little great man taking the stage in a leading part, all nature, beauty of art and the pulse of life. Some of us like to think that the preparation precludes the spontaneity, but it is not so. It is quite the other way. When all the drilling and milling is over, the freedom and the go have nothing to think of but themselves. I found the benefit of that when I learned, rehearsed and played *Forget-me-not* in exactly one week.

One thing that helped me in my work with Regnier was my mastery of the idiom. I began my acquaintance with it at such an early age that I never had an opportunity of making a muddle of it.

The Frenchman is slow to concede that kind of proficiency to any foreigner. He affects to detect a twang in the French of Brussels and of Geneva just as I always felt there was something to be desired in the English of Madame Ristori. She, I think, had the same misgiving. She was in Paris at the time of my visit there for the lessons, and she was glad of my help with the accent of her Lady

Both Sides of the Curtain

Macbeth in the original, as distinct, of course, from her wonderful conception of the part.

Soon I had to pass in both tongues before a full house at the Porte St. Martin. It was, in a way, a part of my course under Regnier. The theatrical critic of the day, Francisque Sarcey, had initiated in 1877 a series of *matinées* for the representation of foreign masterpieces, Russian, Spanish, Italian and English, in a French translation. *The School for Scandal* and two acts of *Macbeth* were second on the list, and I was in the cast. Sarcey, as fluent a speaker as a writer, if you would only concede him his arm-chair in both capacities, gave a short prefatory sketch of the pieces, and then the curtain went up for the French actors. Regnier, Bornier, author of *La Fille de Roland*, with other celebrities of the French stage and Press, came to the English *matinée* as to the others. Regnier insisted on my delivery of the sleep-walking scene in English.

"If you give it in French," he said, "as you must all the rest of your part, they will have it that you are a Frenchwoman. Now I want to show them what an English-speaking woman can do."

When it was all over Sardou came to offer congratulations, and Sarcey laughingly offered to sign me a diploma as a French actress at once. The correspondents of the English and American papers were equally complimentary. Pierre Berton wrote publicly to confirm the flattering notices of the Paris Press, among them one by Jules Claretie, afterwards director of the "House of Molière."

How I Became an Actress

Years later Got offered me an *entrée* at the Français to take the line of business of Madame Favart.

I wish we had some teaching of the same thoroughgoing kind in England and in America, where, I admit, it would not be so easily done. As it is, each company fights for its own hand. There are no schools in either country; it is all a matter of private teaching, which lacks resources and sometimes authority. The old local stock companies in Manchester, Dublin and, in some measure, Edinburgh, supplied the want, and it is to be regretted that they have virtually disappeared. In later years, however, Benson's company of Shakespearean pupils and actors has taken the place of the old repertory theatre at Bristol—the most famous "nursery" of the profession—under its great manager, Chute. The new repertory theatres in Manchester and Liverpool are doing good work.

The travelling companies from London now carry their pieces, their players, and even their scenery from town to town, leaving the provincial centres little to supply but the supernumeraries. The change was inevitable, no doubt; it was in progress even in the time of Shakespeare; but the local company was a great institution in its prime. Its repertory was immense; it had to be ready at call for any emergency requiring a change of bill. It rehearsed incessantly all the masterpieces of drama, and it reared some of the finest actors, among them the Kembles, Macready, Phelps, Mrs. Kendal, the Terrys, and W. H. Vernon. Macready and Phelps, foreseeing what was coming, were particularly insistent on the need of a national theatre—not as a monopoly, of course, but as a school.

While waiting for that, Phelps staked his fortunes on the project of a house wholly devoted to the finest professional work. I am proud to say I once acted with him. I wish it had been in something better than *The Stranger*, but that was sometimes our fate in those days. Nor was it in his own theatre at Sadler's Wells. There, as he once said, in almost the only public speech of his own making, he for eighteen years gave his patrons the best he could find or offer in the pure art of drama. His friends were at first aghast at the thought of it. They feared that while he might only feign madness in one of his greatest parts he was certainly touched by the complaint in this desperate venture.

Sadler's Wells was then but a suburb of London, almost a slum, and quite out of the beat of playgoers of fashion. He persevered, and with the result, as he modestly put it at the end of his management, that he had "paid his way and brought up his family." His audiences never failed him. Many of them never went to any other theatre. He gave them one-and-thirty plays of Shakespeare alone, working through the whole list every six years and then beginning all over again to meet the needs of a new rising generation. This established an intimate personal relation between the audience and the whole company, not excepting its eminent chief. The gallery, at least, usually referred to the characters of the piece by the real names of the actors. An old theatre-going friend of mine used often to

Photo: London Stereoscopic Co.

AS MRS. HALLER IN "THE STRANGER."

tell me of a talk he once overheard in the train. The speaker was understood to be inducting a neophyte into the mysteries of the plot of *Hamlet*. It ran somewhat in this way :

" You see, old Phelps's father was old Marston, king of a place called Denmark. You've heerd of Denmark Street, Soho? Well, keep that in your 'ead. Well, old Marston, he's supposed to have gone off very sudden before the piece begins, and people had their thoughts about it—specially old Phelps. But he sez nothing, until who should turn up one night but Marston's ghost ! He's come to give old Phelps the straight tip that it was a case of murder, and that the chap as did it was his own brother, who's now come in for the crown and all the property, includin' the widder. D'ye foller me, mate? The wust of it was, it was all done so quick that she 'ardly 'ad time to change 'er weeds for the orange blossoms—in fack, the cold scran from the funeral was ackshally served up for the weddin' breakfast. ' Wicked, I call it,' sez old Marston, and so said all of us. ' But, mind,' he sez, ' don't you say nothin' sarcey to Mrs. Warner '—I think it was 'er when I first see it—' your pore mother, an' my misguided wife. If you do you'll 'ear from me sure's you're born. Leave 'er to 'Evin,' he sez. But you should 'ave 'eard old Marston say it : reg'lar upset yer, it did. With that, old Phelps goes clean dotty, or pretends to, anyway ; betwixt and between, as you might say. This gives a awful upset to Sally Atkisson (Atkinson), a gal he was very far gone on before his father's death and she on 'im—' the

same to you and many of 'em,' as you might say;
and she gets wrong in 'er 'ead too. I once cried
over 'er, an' I don't care who knows it, but I'll
tell yer about that bimeby. Well, old Marston, he
sez to old Phelps, you've got to serve that uncle o'
yours same as he served me; I shall keep comin'
back till yer do it—see?"

And so on for the entire plot. For all the home-
liness of speech, there was no vulgarity of thought
or feeling. The piece had gripped the man to his
heart's core, as a mighty personal adventure of the
souls of the players in the tragedy of life.

My reception in Paris brought many offers from
English managers, and I was happy to accept one
that brought me again to the city in which I had
made the first success of my career. In the summer
of 1877 I played Queen Katharine in Manchester,
and in Charles Calvert's great and, I may say, historic revival of *Henry VIII*. The same city and
the same house.

There was something better still to follow: my
own country wanted me at last. In 1878 I recrossed
the ocean, under contract with Jarrett and Palmer,
for what proved to be a triumphant tour of the
United States. But this is for another part of my
story. Dear old Regnier gave me the parting word.
"Good-bye, Ristori, adieu, Rachel, since it is thus
that England speaks of you; but for me, adieu,
Geneviève Ward." Some flatteries seem to come
straight from the heart.

CHAPTER V

HOME AND OUT AGAIN

MISS WARD had "made her proofs" in Europe, and the time had come for an American tour. Her own country, as we have seen, had been at first as shy of the untried actress as England, but now, amply furnished with pieces which had stood the test, she had it all her own way. Three of these, Wills's *Jane Shore*, Shakespeare's *Henry VIII.* and *Macbeth*, served for the whole first part of the tour.

She reached America in July, 1878, accompanied by her father, now growing infirm, and opened with *Jane Shore*, a piece originally written for Miss Heath, and played in England for two or three years with success.

Lewis Wingfield was useful as ever in the designing of dresses for all three plays. Nothing connected with the stage came amiss to him. He could write a piece, play in it, criticise it, scheme the costumes and give precious hints as to the scenery, which all made for unity of effect. He was the forerunner of Percy Macquoid, a painter in the first instance, who brings his knowledge of that art into the others. The dresses especially ought never to be left solely to the costumier.

Both Sides of the Curtain

Her first appearance was at Booth's Theatre in New York, and Press and public were equally satisfied. There was here and there an exception, of course; one writer thought her death of Queen Katharine too realistic, and contrived to turn it into a reproach that, as an admirer had put it, "she actually dies." The suggestion was that she had walked the hospital as part of her professional studies.

"I have never seen anyone die in my life," she says, "but I did take counsel with a doctor of my acquaintance as to symptoms, and on his advice I ceased to trouble about them and to do nothing but 'just die.' I filled my mind with the idea that life and I were parting with mutual content for a 'good morning' in another clime. When it was all over I hardly knew, for a few moments myself, whether I had not really given up the ghost."

By chance Wills came into our talk one day in connection with his place in the programme. "Poor Wills!" she said.

I could but echo her "Poor Wills!" for I, too, had known him well. "If only he could have put himself into a play it would have been his masterpiece in character parts."

"But, then, he would have had to be able to see himself."

I agreed. "Think of him in a box, consciously shedding tears over one of his own pieces, with scalding drops falling into the pit, and now and then a gargantuan sob for the benefit of the rest of the house. He was the last of the Bohemians of literature—because he had not the slightest idea that he was of their number. It came to him from within. He simply lived on lines of least resistance, as indeed we all do. But his preferences in this way led him to get up in the morning in almost the same clothes as those in which he had gone to bed at night. He combed his hair with his fingers, he lit his own fire as often as not, and he sat crooning over it with the sorry cheer of a crust and his pipe until it was time to begin to write on the margin of the first scrap of paper that came to hand."

"As to margins," she said, "when he wrote *Sappho* for me in Dublin we were in full rehearsal before I could get a sight of the final scene. When it came at last, it ended only in a few lines pencilled round the edge of a torn letter, and in Greek, if you please, to bring down the curtain. 'That'll fetch 'em,' he said, 'one of her finest fragments.'"

"I can cap that. Did you ever hear of his summer outing at Etretat? He took a play down there to finish, and was immediately surrounded, as he always was, by a bevy of charming and refined women, drawn to him by their sheer sense of his want of mothering rather than wifing. They took down his work in dictation, they saw that he was properly fed, they tidied him up for their tea-parties, and sometimes sent him out for a ride, or took him, which was the surer way. One morning he was packed off by himself to Havre, a couple of hours' amble, and he was to be back for tea, at which he was usually, much against the grain, on show. But instead of using up all his leave, he reappeared in less than an hour to the astonishment of his lady helps. What had happened? He was utterly unable to explain until someone suggested that he must have left it all to the horse. Working on this line of cross-examination, they found that he had some faint idea of having half-turned the beast to get the wind in his favour in lighting his pipe, and neglected to complete the operation.

"His courtships were the best joke of all. He had proposed to each of his ministrant angels in turn, and then 'taken it back' in sheer terror of the prospect of an ordered life. All knew it, of course, and bore no malice, but this did not preclude a generous revenge. When their evidence of breach of promise was complete they laid it before him at a tea-party, specially convened, and asked him not to make a fool of himself again."

"They might, at least, have had him whipped through the town," mused Geneviève Ward.

"Of course, before he left the place he contrived to lose the manuscript of the play in hand, but the town crier got it back for him, and he wasn't a penny the worse, for somebody else paid the fee. For that matter, his money always went as it came, to anyone who could pitch him a tale of woe.

"His passion was art. He was a painter of sorts. He once received a command from Windsor for a sitting from one of the royal grandchildren. He was among the very few pastellists then in England, and Queen Victoria had been urged to try him in the new style. His answer was by telegram:

Home and Out Again

' Very sorry—engaged.' The Queen laughed gently over that to the last.

"How was it to end? Only in one way, almost as a matter of course, death in a hospital and a funeral service attended by most of the survivors of the breach of promise tea-party, all shedding abundant tears."

Geneviève Ward's Katharine of Aragon was an assured success. She was always happier in herself and in her audiences when dealing with Shakespeare's parts. This was mainly the early training, but it was also due to a certain impatience of melodrama which she never wholly lost. Her Queen Katharine, and her Lady Macbeth after it, filled Booth's Theatre to the topmost bench. Among the inevitable letters from all sorts and conditions, for which stars of the stage are not always to be envied, was one from a young painter of promise who was entirely deaf, and who had consequently to take all his impressions from sight alone. For him *Henry VIII.* was but one gorgeous gesture play, like that revived some years later, on the French stage, as a kind of pendant to the songs without words of musical art. It is astonishing how much may be done in this way. His letter to Miss Ward showed that he had hardly missed a single point, though for many of them she had relied on the voice alone. Ristori's letter was a tribute of quite another sort, all the flow and feeling of the Italian style. "I felicitate you on your grand success which will, I know, augment; and in the end your triumph will be complete over all annoyances which, after all, you must have naturally foreseen. . . . Have me in your heart with the friendship I bear you. Your Adelaide Ristori (Del Grillo)."

Harold Frederic, himself only just coming into the sunlight of acknowledged powers, and hardly so much as that, for he was still but a provincial journalist, had his say—one half, appreciation of the actress, the other, a lament over his own obscurity in Utica: "As a matter of course, dramatic criticism in the country must rest under as many disadvantages as most dramatic representation. What the latter lacks in force of surroundings, in scenery, in the spirit which a crowded and cultured metropolitan house inspires, the former also loses from lack of time, from infrequent requisition, and from the hurry of the slender-staffed daily." Evidently he had New York and London in his dreams. And he was altogether in the right of it; for some things that a big city gives without effort are to be had in no smaller sphere. The fly on the chariot wheel had at least illusions of power denied to the fly on the one-horse shay.

The greater ones were more than gracious. Longfellow bubbled over with praise; in fact, all Boston was moved, and that, of course, included Holmes. Nay, it went further and brought a tribute from Emerson, part of it an invitation to his house and part a copy of verses:

"Oh what is heaven but the fellowship
Of minds, that each can stand against the world
By its own meek and incorruptible will."

AS QUEEN KATHARINE IN "HENRY VIII."

Home and Out Again

Her Queen Katharine naturally brought back memories of Charlotte Cushman, with whom, from mere delicacy of feeling and respect for a great name, Geneviève Ward did not care even to seem to invite comparison. In fact, when it was proposed that she should make her first appearance in *Henry VIII.* she took care to lead off with *Jane Shore.* However, comparisons were made, for they were inevitable, and the happy mean was found by the lady who liked Geneviève Ward's Lady Macbeth as much better as she liked Charlotte Cushman's Queen Katharine.

There was a strange similarity, not so much, if at all, in the genius of the two players as in the mere circumstances of their lives. Both began as singers, both came to grief by trying to do too much with their voices, with the result of incurable overstrain. Both felt the tremendous allurement of Europe. In Geneviève Ward's case it was Paris. There was a certain identity in their taste for pieces. Charlotte Cushman astonished the whole English-speaking world with her Meg Merrilies, carrying it to heights of dramatic power certainly never dreamed of by Scott himself. Both won their way quite as much by character as by genius—that is, by the determination to succeed. Both had the same passion for the stage even in later life. These sympathies naturally brought them together as friends, and the older woman always spoke with generous confidence of the younger's career.

They were different in their fortunes. Charlotte Cushman in London had almost to go begging from

stage door to door to get the chance of a hearing.
What a scene when she called at the Princess's to
beg for an engagement, with at first no better recommendation than her indifferent dressing and her
general first impression of want of charm! The
manager was obdurate, and he was persistently
bowing her out when she threw herself on her knees
and raised her clasped hands: "I know I have
enemies in this country, but, so help me, God, I
will defeat them!" With that evidence of power
the engagement followed as a matter of course, until
she was able to write to her mother: "All my successes put together since I have been on the stage
would not come near my success in London."
Geneviève Ward might have said the same thing of
Paris when she played Lady Macbeth in French to
the satisfaction of the most fastidious audience in
the world.

Both had the same devotion to their calling.
"I think I love and revere all arts equally," wrote
Charlotte Cushman—after Campbell, if you like,
but in simpler and finer form—"only putting my
own just above the others because in it I recognise
the union and culmination of all. To me it seems
as if when God conceived the world, that was
poetry; He formed it, and that was sculpture; He
coloured it, and that was painting; and then, crowning work of all, He peopled it with living beings,
and that was great, divine, eternal drama."

The two differed only, and radically, in their preparation for their work. With Charlotte Cushman,
owing to the more adverse circumstances of early life,

tuition had to come as it might. Her career, to the very last, was one long process of self-education: Geneviève Ward was always the trained artist. She was of the French school, while the other was of the school of nature and circumstance. The difference holds good of some of the writers who inspired them—Corneille, Racine, Molière always knowing exactly what they wanted to do; Shakespeare knowing but just what he had to do, however it came to him. Charlotte Cushman's entire concept of the Meg Merrilies came to her in a flash of insight; under the French system it would have reached her as a part of the curriculum. Diderot's famous Paradox turns on much the same question. Is the actor to identify himself with his parts on the stage, or only to render them in the terms of such identification by incessant study? Is he, in fact, to be dependent on his feelings for his finest effects and not on his perceptions? Coquelin notoriously held that he had no use for real tears. Sarah Bernhardt probably never shed a real tear in the way of business in all her life. On the other hand, Ellen Terry has shed many in her parts. So has Mrs. Kendal.

"What do you think?" I once asked Geneviève Ward.

"I think that Mrs. Kendal may do as she likes; she is a great artist, the greatest of our time. So, for that matter, may either school, according to temperament and training. Both methods may be abused. Clara Morris objected to long runs because she couldn't cry over the same people by the month and year, and she had to fall back on her private sorrows to keep up the supply. Why take so much trouble? The ' tears that live in an onion ' would be an unfailing resource.''

Engagements already contracted in London and in Paris compelled her to suspend the American tour and return to Europe in 1879. She had thought of producing *Henry VIII.* in Paris, and an engagement was ready for her. But the lack of time for carrying it out put an end to that scheme. They wanted her to rehearse and mount the piece in a fortnight. This was impossible in the exceptional circumstances of an English classic introduced to a French audience, and she refused point-blank. Her old master, Regnier, fully approved.

So in August she made straight for London to prepare *Zillah*, by Palgrave Simpson, as her new play. She took the Lyceum while Mr. Irving was away on his summer holiday, and there was no want of care and expense as to scenic effects and costume. It was a dead failure, and was so worried and badgered and torn to pieces by the critics and the public that, after four nights, Miss Ward removed it without protest or complaint as a bad throw of the dice.

Bram Stoker came to her rescue with sound practical counsel: '' You have now to play at once something that you are sure of, to efface with all speed the recollection of a fiasco, of which, happily, you are clearly the victim and not the cause. Should you close now, even for a night, it will be a sign of weakness, theatrically speaking, and a very grave error in judgment. If Lucrezia is not possible

Home and Out Again

Thursday, why, then, Saturday, but to the earnest and broad-shouldered all things are possible."

Lucrezia Borgia was made possible by putting it on in four days, with a company that, with the sole exception of herself, had never seen a line of the play.

Of course, it was only a stop-gap. She was still looking out at all points of the compass for the play of her dreams, and at last it came to her, as such things are apt to do, without any contrivance of her own. Herman Merivale and a collaborator, Mr. Grove, offered her *Forget-me-not*. The joint authors were quite as much in need of a customer as she was in need of a piece. They had failed to find one anywhere for seven long years, and no wonder, for, on the surface, their drama bore no indication of what it might be made to mean. It was far from faultless in construction, but that might be set right, and, for the main thing, it offered her an opportunity she had long sought. She showed it to Bram Stoker, whose judgment in such matters was almost unerring, and on his approving nod she bought, rehearsed and produced it in a single week, while playing Lucrezia all the time, going up and down to the theatre twice a day and learning her own part in her cabs. It was, perhaps, the greatest feat of her whole career, and that is saying much. Her terms of purchase gave her the lease of the sole rights of production for a period of five years, and with option of five years more. In that time the piece had made her fortune in every sense of the word.

Its heroine, the Marquise Stephanie de Mohri-vart, is a woman with a past, of which she has

G   81

tired, and who has determined to win her way into reputable society by sheer strength of will. Her late husband, the noble marquis, a most deplorable person in his later years, had kept a gaming house in Paris, and she had acted as decoy for him until her ambition, and even her interests, led her to think that she might do better in decent society. It was no easy matter, even for her, for the past in question had traces of blood in it. One of her victims at the gaming-table was a Corsican of good family whom she had lured into the house by the promise of a more than friendly interest in him, which did not prevent her from helping to get him kicked out of it when he had lost all his money. He returned to the premises when all was still, stabbed the marquis fatally as he lay in bed, and left his sleeping partner with a wound serious enough to make him believe the subsequent report of her death. He was tried for the crime, and though he had the benefit of extenuating circumstances, was condemned to the galleys for life.

Stephanie now gave up business with a light heart, and set out for Italy, carrying with her the forget-me-not as her favourite flower, to make good her boast that she had the knack of leaving a lasting remembrance on all she met. She had laid her plans with some care. In Rome lived two English ladies who, while they were perfectly blameless in their lives, had yet a secret in *their* past which she unfortunately shared. The secret was simply this: one of them, Rose, in better times, had married Stephanie's son, the Vicomte de Brissac, but had now become a widow by his premature death. The parents had refused their consent to the union; and as this had taken place within the period to which their right of refusal ran, the marriage would now be null and void unless the survivor chose to relent at the eleventh hour. She had only to give publicity to these facts to have both ladies at her mercy— Rose, as widow who had been no wife, the other, Alice, for her sister's sake.

Armed in this way, the adventuress descends on the unhappy pair without an invitation, tells them that she has come for a nice long stay, and that, in the course of it, she expects an introduction to their extremely select visiting circle. It is a terrible dilemma; they cannot comply in justice to their friends, they cannot refuse without absolute ruin to themselves. At this juncture they are so fortunate as to find the friend in need in a clever diplomat on the retired list, Sir Horace Welby, who has just arrived in Rome. Alice confides in him, and he takes up the case with real relish, as he has more than a sneaking kindness for his client.

The play is the duel between Sir Horace and the adventuress. The first passes in the encounter are entirely in the latter's favour. The adversaries grow frank with each other, and when he has at last to tell her what he thinks of her, she is equally candid at his expense. He has kept no gambling hells or anything of that sort, but he has lived his life in the generally accepted way of his sex, and has done some things without blame, which she, as a woman, would have been unable to do without absolute ruin. What is the difference between them after all?

The situation now calls for stronger measures. He must find out some way of compelling her to cut and run. Chance favours him by the arrival of the Corsican of the earlier story, pardoned and free, and now a dependent on Sir Horace, who has generously undertaken to help him to recover his good name. While still believing Stephanie to be beyond the reach of his vengeance, he would be only too glad to discover his mistake. His astute patron seizes the opportunity and resolves to tell Stephanie that her deadly enemy is in Rome, though still ignorant of her presence there, and that if she remains her life may not be worth a moment's purchase. She at first laughs this off as a mere trick, but when he draws a curtain and the figure of the assassin—who is simply waiting his turn for an audience—appears in the moonlit garden beyond, she suddenly gives way, almost on her bended knees, and implores him to save her. He knows that, if she does not impugn the marriage of her son, within a certain time, she will lose all right to do so; and her dread of her pursuer is so powerful that she can only think of flight. She is about to leave the house when the dreaded shape returns on some trivial commission, and still all ignorant of her identity, turns aside at the bidding of her preserver to enable her to leave unobserved. With that she passes out into the void, leaving Alice and her preserver hand in hand.

R. W.

CHAPTER VI

"FORGET-ME-NOT" AND ITS FORTUNES

FORGET-ME-NOT, although with that Geneviève Ward toured the world, was not exactly
a perfect piece. It would be difficult to revive it
in our day, perhaps because it so perfectly suited
its own day. It has had so many successors that
it has got into the category of things we are all
trying not to do now, things belonging to the stagecraft of the Sardou play made with hands. To the
last Regnier maintained that it must have been
French in its origin, and could not have originated
in the brain of an Englishman. "I don't know
where your author found it, but he got it from
us." It was a tribute to the fine mechanism of
its clockwork. Everything in it seemed to come
just where it was wanted. Situations hung on the
very seconds hand. The last scene especially, when
Stephanie passes within a few feet of the man whose
one wicked longing left is to kill her, was regarded
in theatrical circles as the neatest thing of its kind
ever done; this in spite of the fact that the Corsican
was anything but convincing as a bit of human
nature.

Then it had an attraction of a different and
higher kind: as a character play—and Miss Ward

raised it to that level—it was a sheer glorification of the human will. The latest German philosophy on the subject had already come to us in book form, and now here it was in a real live way, with a heroine who seemed to carry her part in it with the sense of a mission.

With all that there were not wanting compensations for the old playgoer who, in modern days, requires and receives more consideration than the young. Stephanie has her moments of yearning tenderness, when she remembers that there was a time when she might have been a good woman.

The very sex grievance came into it, and not as to the weary listener of our day, but to one quite ready to be shocked into repentance for the crime of being a man. Imagine the force of this by an actress who had learned her art in France.

"Why may a man live two lives when a woman must stand or fall by one? What was the difference between us, Sir Horace Welby, in those bygone years, that should make me now a leper and you a saint? There would be no place in creation for such women as I, if it were not for such men as you."

Finally, there was the charm of being called to order by a beautiful woman, mistress of every resource of her art, and especially of its note of scorn. It was a subtly compounded dish. Geneviève Ward and she alone saw what might be made of it; and when she ceased to play it its doom was sealed. Think of the ingenuous young person who once proposed to play it as a soubrette, sitting on a table and smoking cigarettes!

It was a success immediate and complete. The audiences rose to it with their instinctive sense of the acceptable thing, and it never failed her in its power of attraction from August 21, 1879, the day of its appearance, to the end of its phenomenal career.

Letters poured in from all quarters. " I have been happy in your triumph," wrote Ristori. " You have finally passed the Rubicon. I have always said, I will always say, you deserve to win the fullest fortunes for your perseverance, tenacity and indefatigable study. Now at last, you see, you are walking the road of the few, wearing the mantle of greatness."

The English notices were a chorus of praise. One of them struck the same note as Madame Ristori in divining the actress's secret of success. " Not a movement, not a gesture is there which is not carefully thought out. The whole affords an instance of that patient elaboration to which the highest results in art are due." " The study of the fated Stephanie," wrote another, " is rounded, finished, polished and made thoroughly convincing. Fanciful people will complain that Stephanie is a wicked woman, and as such has no right to pose as a heroine of drama. They will gather up their moral skirts and wonder what interest can be attached to the ambition, the hesitation, the defeat and the despair of this proud, cold and passionless beauty. But those who love fine acting and good art will here find a study most worthy of contemplation, from the time that Stephanie glides, serpent-like, upon the scene to the saddened hour when, crushed, humiliated, broken and paralysed with fear, she crouches at the presence of the would-be instrument of her doom and totters forth a wreck and ruin. In cold and defiant sarcasm Miss Ward is excellent to a fault. In the expression of a just and righteous indignation, as when she lashes with her tongue the selfishness and cowardice of her wretched enemy, man, she is exalted and absolutely convincing. In her physical fear she is horribly true. But it is in the passages when the better nature is struggling with a studied indifference, when acting is fighting with reality, when the woman has resolved that the mind and the heart are striving for mastery, that Miss Geneviève Ward gives her best tribute to art."

The piece was played at the Lyceum but sixteen times, under the terms of the agreement with Mr. Irving, but it was immediately taken to the provinces and kept on tour till the end of the year. It returned to town, to the Prince of Wales's Theatre, exactly six months to the day after its first production, with the London verdict fully confirmed.

The French correspondents in London wrote letters about it to their papers. The actors flocked to it as well as the public—the Bancrofts, the Kendals, the Hares were all in the house at one performance, and their greetings behind the curtain were afterwards described by Mr. Kendal as the fourth act of *Forget-me-not* in a full cast. George Eliot sent a friend to sound the actress on behalf

IN "FORGET-ME-NOT."

of a play of her own, *Armgart*, and intimated that
her highest aspirations would be satisfied if she could
see Miss Ward in the part. Oscar Wilde wrote a
letter characteristic in more than one sense of the
word: "If you are not too busy to stop and drink
tea with a great admirer of yours, please come on
Friday, at half-past five, to 18 Salisbury Street.
The two beauties, Lady Lonsdale and Mrs. Langtry,
and Mamma and a few friends are coming." And
"Mamma" wrote a little later: "Mr. Forbes
Robertson was here yesterday; he is very charming,
and admires your genius enthusiastically. Mr.
W. G. Wills was also here, and spoke much of you.
You have waked me to new life." Poor old lady!
She was beginning to need very much awakening at
that time. She had fallen into the sere and yellow
leaf, not only of mere old age, but of a sense of
misgiving as to the future, and it was her hard fate
to live to know the worst.

Royal patronage came early in the run. The
Prince of Wales—King Edward yet to be—saw the
piece twice in a fortnight, and his praise took the
delicate form of general interest in the professional
career of the artist. On his first visit he came to
the green room, and, after complimenting her
warmly on the performance, and especially on her
French in certain phrases of the dialogue, urged her
to play a French drama in London, and suggested
L'Aventurière. On a subsequent visit in the same
quarter, after the play, he was accompanied by the
Duke of Edinburgh and Duke of Teck. Miss Ward's
little dog, who was in the room, playfully welcomed

the Duke by snapping at his heels, and his mistress called out, " Come here, Teck ! " Both the Princes exchanged glances, but Miss Ward, taking in the situation at a glance, explained. " My dog's name is Teck—short for Thekla—a German character in one of my plays." The favourite had its basket at the theatre as one of the properties ; and it was now, " Basket, Teck ! " This seemed to tickle Albert Edward's fancy ; he chuckled, " Basket, Teck ! Basket, Teck ! " to his cousin as he went downstairs. The Prince went further in his kindness and attended a private entertainment at Hamilton Aïdé's, at which Miss Ward played in a French piece with M. Marius.

Meanwhile, the French performance in London had been arranged, and she crossed to Paris to rehearse *L'Aventurière* with Regnier, and play it in time to enable her to return to London without breaking the run of her successful piece.

The provinces took up the chorus of praise before they had seen the play. Russell, of Liverpool, wrote of her in one of those searching and profound pamphlets on the art of the theatre by which he had helped to found the reputation of Irving. Italy even had its part in the celebration. A manager there suggested an engagement in which she was to play with Salvini, in Salvini's own language, which she spoke as well as she spoke French.

Yet it was not altogether an unclouded sky. Merivale and Grove, the authors of *Forget-me-not*, were disquieted by the very success of it. Their eagerness in trying to get the better of their bar-

gain recalled the story of the Hebrew who, when
a buyer had closed with his first price, committed
suicide on the galling reflection that he might have
asked more. They allowed her to go on with the
mounting of the play, after they had orally accepted
the agreement, as it stood ready for signature. So
on the day of production everything was ready
for the raising of the curtain, everything with one
exception—the signatures. In the afternoon they
came down to the theatre with a proposal for a revision. She absolutely refused to listen to anything
of the sort, or even to raise the curtain till she had
the signatures. The curtain was raised.

More difficulties supervened. When Merivale
first offered the play to Miss Ward, he wrote to
call her attention to the fact that a subordinate
character named Rose had been cut out. She
assented to this, as the character was not required
in the cast as distinct from the mere allusions to it
in the dialogue. Afterwards, when the piece was
brought out at the Lyceum, he asked her to include it
in the cast, as he wished to provide a part for a lady
in whom he was interested. This was done to oblige
him. But when the piece was removed to the Prince
of Wales's Theatre Miss Ward excised it once more,
as a matter perfectly within her discretion. With
that he applied for an injunction to prevent her from
performing the piece. The case came before Lord
Coleridge, and Miss Ward's counsel was able to show
that the piece had been leased without the character.
and to hand up a copy in which the part was struck
out in pencil by Merivale himself. A letter was also

produced in which he said the play was much too lengthy, and was improved by the omission. The only answer the plaintiff had to make was that his partner, the joint author, did not agree with this view. This was Spenlow and Jorkins with a vengeance, and the motion was refused with costs.

Meanwhile, by way of having a second string to her bow for provincial tours, Miss Ward produced *Annie Mie* at the Prince of Wales's Theatre. *Annie Mie* was a Dutch piece, and the actress thought there were hopes of it, but she was soon undeceived, though it had every chance in public expectation on the first night. The Prince and Princess of Wales were present, but so also was the Press, and its unanimous verdict was that *Annie Mie* would never do for the London stage.

"You are admirable in *Annie Mie*," wrote Sala, the constant friend, "but it is a great way below your artistic capacity, and in the play there are gallons too many tears, and at least eight mourning coaches too many. I have been obliged to say so in my public criticisms, doing justice to your own genius and dramatic insight, but into the part itself I have been bound to pitch, and I hope you know I am too true a friend of yours to say what I do not mean."

The letter was quite honourable to both sides, for Miss Ward took it as it was meant. So *Annie Mie* disappeared from the London boards for ever.

The very day after, Miss Ward was on her way to America, for Merivale had engineered another big push by leasing her successful play for the United

"Forget-me-not" and its Fortunes

States to Lester Wallack and a subordinate agent named Moss. He knew that in renting it to Miss Ward as an American actress, her highest hopes of it had been founded on the approval of the American public. It was essentially a part of the tour which was to mark her triumphant return to her own country. He now affected to believe that their contract related to Great Britain alone, and claimed the right to put the character, which she had created, up to auction for the whole American stage-world. It was this, and the need of immediate action which it imported, that sent her at such headlong speed on board the steamer. On her arrival she issued the following notice to "managers, actors and the public" for immediate publication in the journals of the Union:

"I have crossed the ocean at this inclement season to protect my purchased rights of exclusive production of *Forget-me-not* against the deliberate piracy of Lester Wallack and Theodore Moss. I am preparing papers for an injunction against them, and shall push my legal redress with vigour. Meanwhile, I beg to say that neither Mr. Wallack nor Mr. Moss has any right to *Forget-me-not*, and, further, I will enjoin every manager and actor in the country not to attempt to play my piece. I have this day concluded to play the piece in all the large cities, beginning in the City of New York at an early date.—GENEVIÈVE WARD."

The cable, of course, had not been idle on the part of the offender. Miss Ward sailed on December 11 and arrived on December 22, only to learn

93

that Wallack had been four days ahead of her by producing the piece on December 18—removing a highly successful play to make room for it.

She at once applied for the threatened injunction. Her whole future, as she felt, lay in her hold on this drama. It was for her the tide in the affairs of men. With it she could tour the world, without it all was uncertainty. She rose to the occasion, and, with a slight paraphrase, it may be said to have been a case of "Venus all entire clinging to her *play*."

Her litigation was pushed with all imaginable energy, and it soon came before the court, with all its apparatus of pleadings, examinations, "exhibits," as they are called in America, and what not. One exhibit was an extract from the original agreement which ran as follows: "The authors, who are the owners of the copyright of the play called *Forget-me-not*, hereby agree that the purchaser shall have the sole right to produce for her own performance the said play in English, as written by them, for a period of five years from the 21st August, 1879, with a right of renewal for a further period of five years upon precisely similar terms." It was difficult to reconcile this with another exhibit in the following words: "We, Florence Crawford Grove and Herman Charles Merivale, &c. &c., do, in consideration of the sum of one dollar, hereby transfer, assign set over and convey to Theodore Moss of Wallack's Theatre New York all our rights title and interest in and for our play *Forget-me-not* in and throughout the United States of America."

"Forget-me-not" and its Fortunes

The only plea they had to offer was that, as British authors, they had no rights outside their own country to give, and consequently that the sole right which they had leased to Miss Ward could not carry any sort of right in America. All that they had sold to her was the right to play it within the British jurisdiction, a wretched subterfuge—for from the very first there had been no concealment of her intention to take it to the United States. In their pleadings on this point they put on an air of contemptuous ignorance of the ways of a wicked generation by humbly confessing: " We are not good at what is known and admired in the modern dramatic world as smartness."

In his examination before the court, Mr. Moss showed an extraordinary reluctance to commit himself on any point. The plain answer to the plain question seemed to have no attraction for him.

Question.—" Do you claim an interest in the play *Forget-me-not* ? "—Objected to; answered subject to objection : " I do."

Question.—" When did you acquire that right? " —Objected to, but answered subject to compulsion : " Verbally in 1878."

Question.—" Does your title to the play arise by purchase thereof? "—Objected to, but answered subject to objection : " It does."

Question.—" Was such purchase evidenced by any memorandum in writing? "—Objected to, but answered : " The purchase was both verbally and in writing."

Both Sides of the Curtain

Question.—" Will you produce it on examination and show it to me as counsel for Miss Ward?"— Objected to, and answered subject to objection : " I will not, unless ordered by the court."

Question.—" Have you got a copy of the play in your possession? "—Objected to, &c. : " I have."

Question.—" Is the copy in your possession in print? "—Objected to, &c. : " It is in print."

All went well in the end. By January 7 Miss Ward had got her injunction, and Lester Wallack and his partner were compelled to withdraw the piece from the stage. From that time forward the lessee had a free run with it. A month later it was produced by her in Boston, with Longfellow in the audience on first night. In September of the same year it began a long tour which brought it to New York, where it reached its 600th representation, with a stage ceremonial suited to the occasion.

What a change now in all the tenor and outlook of her life! There were no more icy letters from managers belonging to the time of her earlier struggles, even when she had made her name. Lord Newry, for instance, had written in 1876 to express his sense of shock at the demand of £40 a week for a salary :

" I am glad for your sake that your prospects in Paris are so good that you cannot feel yourself justified in relinquishing them under a less sum than £40 a week. I am surprised at your mentioning such a sum "—no wonder, for it meant much more then than it means now—"for you know that there is not one single lady in London drawing that salary, and not more than four at the outside in receipt of even half of it. It will be waste of time for you to communicate with Mrs. John Wood who has taken my piece. Her salary list is already very large, and I feel she could not accept your terms." However, he wound up on a pleasant note: "I think you will show the Parisians that they are not the only artists in the world."

A little later, after her Lady Macbeth in Paris, Lionel Tennyson wrote:

"MADAM,—Although I know that the opinions of a stranger cannot be otherwise than a matter of indifference to so great an artist as yourself, I cannot refrain from letting you know that I am one of the many who must always be grateful to you for your representation of yesterday."

Russell, of Liverpool, followed in the same encouraging way:

"With all sincerity, and without hyperbole, your Queen Katharine is quite beyond any suggestion of mine. The last act is as fine as anything I recollect, remembering stories of Mrs. Siddons, &c. It did seem to me that with a little more, may I say, 'devil,' you would have frightened the Duke of Buckingham's surveyor more. But the warning was very powerful as it was, and I can well understand your desire to keep well within the rounded grace which is now so seldom witnessed in stage declamation, but of which you have the secret."

The tour ended in May, 1882. The American

H

critical estimates confirmed the public judgment. The best of them, that of the *New York Tribune*, may stand for the rest, though not all were so well written.

"Those who saw *Forget-me-not* at Wallack's Theatre would scarcely know it for the same piece on seeing Miss Ward as the heroine" (Miss Coghlan had performed the pirated part until stopped by the injunction). "Miss Coghlan's rendering was charming for its piquancy and for its volatile, sensuous, mischievous vitality. Miss Ward's performance is brilliant with intellect and character. . . . The points of assimilation between the present actress and the part arise in an imperial force of character, intellect, brilliancy, audacity of mind, iron will, perfect elegance of manners, a profound self-knowledge, and unerring intuition as to the relations of motive and conduct in that vast network of circumstance which is the social fabric. . . . The character is reared not upon the basis of unchastity, but upon the basis of intellectual perversion . . . cold as snow, implacable as the grave, remorseless, wicked, but beneath all this depravity capable at last of self-pity, capable of momentary regret, capable of a little bit of human tenderness, aware of the glory of the innocence she has lost, and thus not altogether beyond the pale of compassion."

The moral estimate must not be omitted, as a note of the criticism of the time. "Art does not go far enough when it stops short merely at the revelation of the felicitous powers of the artist, and it is not altogether right when it tends to beguile

"Forget-me-not" and its Fortunes

sympathy with an unworthy object and perplex the spectator's perception as to good and evil. . . . The added blight likewise rests upon it, though this is of far less consequence to the spectator when it is burdened with moral sophistry. Vicious conduct in a woman, according to Stephanie's logic, is in no way more culpable or disastrous than vicious conduct in a man. . . . But it is hardly necessary to point out that all this is a specious and mischievous perversion of the truth. Every observer, who has looked carefully upon the world, is aware that the consequences of wrong-doing by a woman are vastly more pernicious than those of wrong-doing by a man, that society could not exist in decency if to its already inconvenient coterie of reformed rakes it would add a legion of reformed wantons, and that it is innate wickedness and evil propensity that makes such women as Stephanie, and not the mere existence of the wild young men who are willing to become their comrades and generally end by being their dupes and victims."

With this the praise of the artistry resumes its course.

"Not since Ristori acted Lucrezia Borgia in this country has our stage exhibited such an image of imperial will, made radiant with beauty, and electrical with flashes of passion. The leopard and the serpent are fatal, terrible, and loathsome, yet they scarcely have a peer among nature's supreme symbols of power and grace. In the last scene of *Forget-me-not* the situation is one of the strongest that dramatic ingenuity has invented, and Miss

Both Sides of the Curtain

Ward invests it with a colouring of truth that is pathetic and awful."

In a letter on this passage Garth Wilkinson (the translator of Swedenborg and the supreme authority on his teaching) wrote to the actress: "I am grateful to the writer for also, in his ardent admiration, being so far master of his reason as to be able to declare that human good is the last attainment of the drama in both its parts."

The sweet praise of comrades was not wanting: "the profession" were in line with the public and the Press.

R. W.

CHAPTER VII

HALF ROUND THE PLANET

ON my return from America I toured in England, and I had the good fortune to secure the services of Mr. Vernon as my supporter in the leading parts. He lacked but one thing—push, perhaps—to rank him among the great actors of his time. He had recently toured on his own account with a play called *Mammon*, by Sydney Grundy, with which he made an enormous success. He went to America with Toole, who was going to start him on the piece, but did not; and he came back very much disappointed. My acting manager suggested him for the part of Sir Horace. I had played once with him at the Crystal Palace under Wyndham in *The Hunchback*, and I had heard of him as a great actor. He came to see me and was very nice about accepting what terms I could offer for the small tour with which we started. On the termination of that he engaged to go with me on an autumn tour, and, of course, he had better terms.

After this I came to London and took the Olympic Theatre for six months, with Mr. Vernon as my leading man. We produced there *Forget-me-not*, *The Queen's Favourite*, by Sydney Grundy, *The Great Catch*, by Hamilton Aïdé, and another play, *Rachel*. I also played Medea there, Nance Oldfield and Meg Merrilies.

While playing at the Olympic, Garner, one of the partners of the great firm, Williamson, Garner, and Musgrove, of Australia, who was a friend of Mr. Vernon's, came to see me, and we made an arrangement to go to Australia, with Mr. Vernon as my partner and leading man.

I never met so versatile an actor. He was one —as were Ellen Terry and Madge Kendal—of the old school of Chute's, of Bristol, the hotbed of theatrical success some sixty or seventy years ago, though I do not think Irving was ever there. Vernon was at Chute's for many years, finally as stage-manager. He would play anything, from *Macbeth* to *Cool as a Cucumber*, though he was naturally a comedian. He had played almost all Shakespeare and the old drama, and was an absolutely splendid all-round man and marvellous " study." He told me that in the old days they played as many as twelve five-act pieces in a week. They would come home at night, have their supper, and, as he called it, " swallow " their part in a new play. It was rehearsed next morning and played at night; and this six times a week.

Of course, in those days the awful *matinée* system had not come in, and there were only night performances!

But the tremendous strain told in after years, and when Vernon was about seventy his brain began to fail. He was a fine elocutionist; when we were in doubt about anything of that kind we always went to him. With that, the quickest and best stage-manager I ever worked with. He put up *Tosca* at the Princess's Theatre in one week and played a part himself. Between ourselves, no manager in London could to-day perform the feat—especially as it went without a hitch.

He had a quick ear for all local varieties in dialect. When we arrived in Melbourne he at once challenged the waiter of the hotel as a Gloucestershire man, though the latter was manifestly putting on for metropolitan finish. " Yes, sir," was the humble confession, " and my name is Garge."

The failure of brain power commenced with vertigo when he was playing with Alexander. He was teaching with me at the time, for we had a sort of partnership in a dramatic school. I noticed that, instead of letting the pupils recite to him, he simply read out to them unconsciously. That was the first sign : then, at the end, he had no knowledge of anything, or, saddest of all for his friends, of anyone. He died in 1905.

The Olympic lesseeship was a hard struggle, and I lost a good deal of money, but made up for it in the Australian tour. Yet, if I had not been playing there, Garner very likely would not have seen me, and his name stands in this connection for my great world tour. A curious thing happened when I played Meg Merrilies there. Some relation of Charlotte Cushman's—a brother, I think—wrote me quite an insulting letter about my daring to undertake his sister's great part. I wrote back saying that no one could admire Charlotte

Both Sides of the Curtain

Cushman in it more than I, and that I could only follow her as best I might. Still, I should like him to come and see my modest effort. He did so, and afterwards wrote me a charming letter on his enjoyment of the performance.

She was a grand woman in every way—a fine, intellectual, big-hearted creature, a great tragic actress—and America may be proud of her. She had not had much regular teaching—her genius was innate. She was generous to her fellow actresses, and to me especially; in fact, she told a very dear friend of mine that her mantle had fallen on my shoulders. It was the highest and most stimulating praise I ever received.

I was engaged, with Mr. Vernon as my partner, to play my repertory in Australia. Garner was to furnish locally the general company, the theatre, the scenery and everything. He also engaged Mr. Vernon's son to go with us, and a companion maid for me.

I could have taken my company out—Ristori took hers with her; she had to do so, as they were Italians—but it was more profitable to me not to be bothered with a company when I could find one ready-made. There were very good actresses there indeed. One of them was Patty Brown, who played in *The Amazons* and became quite famous here. She was one of my younger actresses.

We started on December 12, 1888, and went through the Suez Canal to Bombay—a run of over six thousand miles—and, being there, I thought I would not lose the opportunity of seeing India. We

AS MEG MERRILIES IN "GUY MANNERING."

played only once in India, before the Viceroy. I took a trip up country to Jeypore, Delhi, Agra, Cawnpore, Lucknow, Benares, and down to Calcutta, where the performance was at the Viceroy's request. From Calcutta we went by steamer to Madras, where I saw the wonderful Juggernaut car, and to Colombo and Kandy, making our final stop at Colombo to wait for the steamer to Australia. While waiting, we went to Kandy to see the wonderful Buddha's garden temple and his tooth— which looked very much like an elephant's. I asked the priest, much to his consternation, how often they had to renew it, as it was always on exhibition and otherwise open to mischance. It was about two inches long—no man could have had a tooth like that.

At Colombo I gave a performance at the club; there being no stage, we played on tables, which were rather rickety. In Colombo also I saw a Cingalese play. The theatre was in the gardens, an octagonal, with columns open to the air, and lighted by coconut shells with oil and a wick in them. It was not exactly a hall of dazzling light. The prompter, in Cingalese costume, an apron tied round his body, and his long hair flowing down his back, stood beside the hero and prompted every word from the book in his hands.

I once went to a Chinese play in San Francisco, but we had to run away from its realism, as it began with the birth of the hero.

I think Colombo was the hottest place I was ever in. The thermometer is only 88 all the year round, but the rays of the sun are vertical and you have no shadow. If you were to walk across a small courtyard without a helmet, you would have sunstroke. I think that is why the natives wear their wonderful hair long—even the men's is down to their knees—with a comb at the back, and hanging down loose. I was worn out with the heat when I left Ceylon, and I slept straight through for forty-eight hours on the steamer.

There was one curious thing about the Buddha celebration. It was at night in a garden with an open temple. A little boy of ten or so had to recite prayers in a language he did not understand—the Pali—which is to their ritual what Latin is to the Catholic. He had been well coached, for he went on for two hours in his unknown tongue, with no pause and no refreshment beyond an occasional sip of water from the hollow of his hand. It was very impressive, all the women in bright-coloured garments sitting on the ground around the temple, with the men behind them standing, in the moonlight —quite fairylike indeed.

Kandy was once the capital, and one of the great temples was there. The frescoes outside this temple consisted of all the most awful tortures of hell fire that you could imagine. The great beauty of the place is the botanical garden, where all the spice trees and the bamboo trees grow. There is one tree of which each bamboo is about the circumference of a man's thigh, and the group itself must be four or five feet in diameter.

It was all so different in Australia, so British

yet with a difference. The Australians are like the Americans; it is the same with the Canadians—all these people are smarter than the men in England. The audiences were very quick and very much alive. Melbourne was little more than fifty years old when I went there—magnificent buildings and hotels next to little corrugated tin buildings waiting for someone to take the plot and fill in with palaces.

At Albany, our first stopping-place in Australia, I heard that my little dog Thekla, who had been my constant companion for over ten years, would be quarantined. The Australians had passed a law that dogs were to be quarantined for six months and £50 paid for their keep. I at once telegraphed to Mr. Garner to get exemption for my dog, or I should not land. He went to the Premier, who, having a soul both for dogs and drama, agreed to let Thekla remain in my care for quarantine. So that when I arrived in Melbourne my little dog ran down the gangway with me, *free*.

The following year Sarah Bernhardt went to Australia with several animal friends. Not being as determined as I was she did not refuse to land, but paid £50 for each animal, and was deprived of them for six months.

I was asked what I should have done on arrival had the Premier not granted a permit for my dog. I answered I should have gone on from Melbourne to Sydney, and then on the journey back for home returned to Melbourne without landing and made straight for England. If my little dog wasn't good enough for the country the country wasn't good enough for me.

I was not to play for a week or so. To prepare matters I delivered my letters of introduction, one of them to Sir Henry and Lady Lock, through mutual friends in London, and this began a friendship with her that lasts till now.

The Governors are really the royalties of the place, and their patronage is a great help. We began to rehearse, and I had a most efficient company which Mr. Vernon soon drilled into perfection.

Forget-me-not was an enormous success. I do not suppose they ever had such another first night as we had there. The critics were most appreciative; the success of the tour was assured. Our first season in Melbourne ran to about three months, and *The Queen's Favourite* was in our repertory.

Then we went to Sydney to the Theatre Royal, which was under the same management, and opened with *Forget-me-not*, continuing, of course, with our other plays. We gave *Macbeth* there, a very fine production with new scenery and most successful. When we came back to Melbourne we produced *Macbeth* at the Theatre Royal, not at the Prince's, which is a smaller house. The students took the whole gallery and displayed an enormous black flag, embroidered in silk, with their badge—a death's-head. You may imagine the uproar and the enthusiasm. The flag was presented to me, and I have it still—now, as then, an omen of nothing but good.

Next we went to Geelong and played there for

a week; then to Ballarat, and made a small provincial tour, afterwards back to Melbourne, where we took steamer for Launceston, in Tasmania. There we found a very strange little railway which took us to Hobart, the principal place—wonderful vegetation, trees exquisitely beautiful, houses covered with roses, hedges of red geranium three or four feet high.

The roads in Tasmania were all made by the convicts, and were as smooth and fine as any I had seen in France. There is a wonderful mountain in Hobart called Mount Wellington, right on the coast; the roses were in the valley and snow was on the top of the mountain. The curious thing is there is no scent to the roses. My complimentary bouquets from the theatre gave nothing but colour to my drawing-room. There is a saying in Australia that the birds have no song, the bees have no sting, and the flowers no scent—the first and the last are difficult things to do without.

During my stay there I went to the criminal lunatic asylum. Hobart had been one of the great convict settlements, and I saw a most extraordinary man. He was one of the principal figures in the famous book, " For the Term of His Natural Life." He had escaped with a " pal " convict. They got lost in the bush and were starving, and he killed and ate his mate. He was captured, but again escaped with another pal. The description of their watching to see which should kill the other is most thrilling. The first-mentioned was again successful and again captured, and this was the end of his career as a cannibal. He was perfectly insane and a leper, a disgusting sight.

It is generally supposed that Botany Bay was a convict settlement. When I was in Sydney we drove over to it, an exquisite scene, and I asked to see the old penal quarters. I was told that no convict had ever landed there. The first convict ship went to Botany Bay, and some of the officers landed and prospected about bringing the ships in. One or two of them wandered off and came to Sydney Harbour, which is the finest in the world. They immediately returned and reported their discovery; so at Sydney the convicts were landed and there the convict colony was formed. There are still some persons in the place who are the descendants of the old convicts, or "lags," as they were called. One of these was proprietor of a theatre, a very illiterate man, coarse but enterprising. A story is told of him that once, when he was rehearsing a new play, someone criticised the scenery and told him the perspective was wrong. He sent for the scene painter and said: "I didn't limit you to expense; why didn't you get the right perspective? Get another one at once."

After Hobart we had one of our worst journeys —from Hobart to Dunedin, in the South Island, New Zealand, 960 miles. We had storms the whole way, and I was the only one of the company who came into the dining saloon and took the meals. The sailors were convinced that it was because we had a great many missionaries on board. I will tell you a funny story of Mr. Vernon and a drunken missionary in the top berth over him. When Mr. Vernon walked in his fellow-passenger began to say in broken English—but no, I mustn't go on with that. I have a poor opinion of some missionaries. They go with the Bible only in one hand and the whisky bottle in the other, and they destroy the natives. In the Sandwich Islands they told me that the only missionaries who did any good were those who had no personal interest to serve.

We arrived at Dunedin—Scotland overseas you might call it, so many speak with the Scottish accent. It is a beautiful town, with the hotels and everything perfect. We played a month there, and from Dunedin we went up by steamer to Christchurch—190 miles. The steamers always waited for us until we could embark after our last performance at the smaller places on the way. Christchurch—most interesting town—was founded by "the Canterbury Pilgrims," as they are called, prospecting there after the return of Captain Cook. They had to climb the mountains from the coast to get into the valley, where they built Christchurch. It had a beautiful river running through it which was named the Avon. There were no trees, but they planted willows and other English growths, and it is now one of the most exquisite scenes you can imagine. Christchurch now boasts a cathedral. The Government of New Zealand generally resides at Wellington, but was at Christchurch for a time. It is summer there at Christmas time, and the Governor, to whom I had letters of introduction, gave many garden-parties at that season, in which his wife could not share, as she was an invalid confined to her sofa indoors. At one of these parties I was standing with another guest and talking to our host when a lady came up, a very imposing person (the Bishop's wife), with whom I conversed until she left us. On joining another group we heard she had been expatiating on the Governor's wife and saying what a charming woman she was and how delighted she was to have met her. One of the party said:

"I did not know you had been in the Governor's house."

"No more have I."

"Oh, then you cannot have seen the Governor's wife."

"Oh, yes," she said, pointing to me, "and there she is." They all laughed.

"That is Miss Ward, the eminent actress."

The Bishop's wife was so overcome with the thought of such close contact with the stage that she went home, no doubt to receive medical attention.

I am glad to say I heard of no fatal result, though we played there a month.

I did not go to the west coast. They say the fiords there on the South Island are finer than any in Norway.

There were no animals in New Zealand—only birds—until Captain Cook left some pigs and sheep. The birds are very curious: there is one called the kiwi—about the size of a guinea hen. It has no wings, but I believe there are the slight rudiments of them, hardly visible to anything but the eye of faith. In one of the islands they found the bones of an enormous bird—the *moa*—about the size of a camel. An eminent naturalist collected the bones and reconstructed the skeleton. He was then able to make exchanges with European museums, and with these he founded several very beautiful museums in the large towns.

Sheep were then so plentiful that I have seen thousands sold for six shillings a head, and you could get a quarter of lamb in the market for half a crown.

From Christchurch we went to Wellington, in the North Island. The country is mountainous, and on entering the passage into the narrow harbour you are, as it were, imprisoned by the hills.

When we left a storm was raging in the harbour, and many people refused to start and went ashore again. Of course, our company remained on the steamer and went to bed expecting an awful night. We retired to our berths, and a short time after there was a sudden calm, as though we were on a lake. On inquiry we found that we had just left the harbour; the storm was there, but there was none at sea.

From Wellington we went to Napier—oh, the heat was sweltering. We played there for a week, and then sailed to Auckland, another four hundred miles, another gorgeous harbour. Auckland represents the American element; Dunedin, as I have said, the Scottish; Christchurch the English. What Wellington stands for in this way I do not remember, but it is not without distinction of another kind. It must surely be the windiest place in the world. They say a man has to hold his hat on except when he turns a corner of the street, and then he has to hold his head on.

My tour was supposed to end at Auckland. I informed my company that I would take two weeks' rest, after which, if they liked, they could continue with me, and I would make return visits to Dunedin and take them back to Australia. They agreed.

We left Auckland and went to Gisborne by steamer again, where we played a week. The town was very small, but we did well, people coming from up-country forty or fifty miles to see the performances. The fertility of the soil here is quite extraordinary. A fruit garden which had only been laid out six months was beginning to bear, and an apple tree, but the half-year old and four feet high, had already produced an apple that was the size of a small melon. The people there were most hospitable and made our stay delightful—picnics and all sorts of things.

Then we made our way back to Napier, and from there to Christchurch again—890 miles—all were return visits. We went to the Bluff—the furthermost southern point of the southern island—stopping and playing at small towns for one night.

At the Bluff we were regaled with oysters—the only treat of the kind. From there we took steamer to Melbourne—1,200 miles. It was perfect; no missionaries on board and beautiful weather. We did not play in Melbourne, but went from there on the Orient steamer to Adelaide, another 600 miles. We played there a month with great success, returned to Melbourne, and went thence to Sydney and Brisbane. We were coasting, and the seals and porpoises were a feature : there were millions of the latter, some rubbing up against the vessel.

At Brisbane we played about four weeks, and I spent charming times with the Governor's wife, Lady Musgrave, who was an American and a great friend of my cousin's in New York.

The rats were awful. I think Brisbane was one of the worst places I ever came across for them. They sometimes made holes in the ceiling and ran down the walls. Sydney was just as bad ; one night I felt a great rumbling under my pillow—rats! I need scarcely say I jumped out of bed and pushed the electric bell. The porter came up, and I went to my dining-room on the veranda and slept the rest of the night on the dining-table, where the pests could not get at me. I left the hotel the next day, but there was no getting away from them. When I left the theatre in Brisbane I had a man in front of me banging the walls to scare them off, and then had to take a carriage to go one block to my hotel, with the disgusting things squealing all along the road. The steamers were protected by many ingenious devices, but where holes are merely blocked up at night new ones are sure to be found in the morning. The worst was on the steamer when we left. Mrs. Sala told me that she woke up one night and there were fourteen rats in her cabin. I refused to go into my cabin, and the captain kindly gave me the use of his state-room on deck—until 4 A.M., when he had to turn in. Then I was allowed to go up to the chart-room and spend the rest of the night there. I never went into my cabin the whole journey.

From Brisbane we came back to New South Wales, and I played a week in Newcastle, which, like its English namesake, is a great coaling place.

I read the Declaration of Independence at Sydney on July 4 in an enormous tent for the American section, and I paid a return visit there of four weeks.

CHAPTER VIII

THE OTHER HALF

WE were again at Melbourne in August, 1885, and on our arrival on the 3rd, worked hard at the theatre all the afternoon. We had a grand reception, as it was the "command" night. We played there for five weeks and then made a tour in Gippsland, where the swans are as black as the berries on the hedges in England and almost as plentiful. I often think of it when I see them treated as rare birds on our tiny lake in Regent's Park. That's what travel does for one : it kills the sense of wonder, and is both gain and loss. England seems all samples in miniature, particularly the scenery.

At the end of October we returned to Melbourne in race week, the great week of the year. I had previously suggested to Sir Henry and Lady Lock that I should do something to show my appreciation of the way in which I had been received in Australia by giving a performance for some charity —thinking a children's charity would be best. But she said there was one which, though it was not popular, she was much interested in—the building of a wing to the women's hospital, as a lying-in ward. They had only a lean-to for that purpose, with rooms 8 feet by 10 feet with two beds in them, which were never aired even in the intervals of occupancy. It was one patient up, another down—a shocking state of things. In consequence puerperal fever was very prevalent.

I seized the idea at once and set to work, beg, beg, begging till I became the sturdiest of the vagrant clan. I went to the Mayor and got him to lend me the Town Hall for the performance, and the scenery was painted for nothing by our manager. I went to Mr. Mackinnon, of *The Argus*, and asked him to put in a little advertisement for me. The next day there appeared a whole column. He had headed it with £100 for the charity, and would take nothing for the advertisement. That was not all. The piece I chose was *Antigone*—which I had played at the Crystal Palace under Wyndham's management in 1875—and every week until the benefit performance *The Argus* had some article on the subject, either of the Greek drama or of Mendelssohn, who wrote the music, until *Antigone* became the rage. The other papers all followed suit, so I got all my advertisements for nothing. The Philharmonic Society, numbering ninety-five, gave their services for chorus, and even furnished their dresses.

I turned the gallery of the Town Hall into private boxes, which I myself sold, driving round the squatters' warehouses to see these wealthy men. The first on whom I called was Sir William Clark, whose wife was one of the Governors of the hospital. I asked him to take a box. He said :

" With pleasure—how much? "

The Other Half

" One hundred pounds."

" Miss Ward, if I gave you a hundred pounds for a box you would get nobody to give you any-thing else."

" Leave that to me, Sir William "—he was the richest man in the colony—" if you give me a hundred pounds others will give me fifty." This proved absolutely true, for his brother, to whom I went next, though not so open-handed a man, finally agreed to give me fifty, and it was much the same with many others.

I had one or two rather peculiar adventures on this quest. One portly gentleman, by no means a saint to look at, said, when I suggested a hundred pounds :

" I do not believe in it, Miss Ward—it is encouraging vice." All he meant by this pharisaical speech was that the hospital drew no distinction between one class and another in its ministrations. It was accessible not only to respectable women— many of them travelling forty or fifty miles from up-country, where there were no hospitals, and on horseback, to bring their children into the world in Melbourne—but also to poor " unfortunates " in their hour of need.

Well, I am afraid I lost my temper. I rose and I said :

" How dare you say such a thing ! Whose fault is it ? Yours, the men's "—in my most tragic tones.

He gave me a cheque for a hundred pounds.

I was going to lunch with Lady Lock after one of these excursions and told her my adventures, which amused her very much. One wealthy dry-goods man promised a hundred pounds if he might have the box next the Governor's: he had it. The funniest experience was that with a man of Irish descent living in the country in very grand style. I informed him that I came from Lady Lock, and the object of my coming and my name. He flung out of the room, horrified that he had been in the presence of an actress! My parting shaft was, "I will tell Lady Lock how charmingly you received her messenger!" for she had authorised me to use her name in every way. He became the laughing-stock of Melbourne.

The performance took place on November 6. The stalls were all sold on the first day for £800, at £1 each: the boxes I had disposed of long before. Such a rush had never been known. Sir George Verdon, the head of the Scottish Bank there, a very influential man who had been most kind to me throughout, was the treasurer, and he took charge of the proceeds. Nothing passed through my hands; my business was only to bring the money in, leaving others to take care of it. There was a certain narrowness of mind in the community, say what you will. Thanks to that, we had to play at the Town Hall instead of the theatre. Bishop Moorhouse, a large liberal-minded man, afterwards Bishop of Manchester, told me that if I gave the play in a playhouse he would not be able to come. When he first came to Melbourne it was announced that he would attend a theatre for the benefit of a children's hospital, but he received a bushel of letters of protest, one from an old up-country parson, who wrote, "For Christ's sake, don't go." He had to comply, or he would have lost all his influence and power.

They wanted £5,000 to build the wing—and I made in money £2,680 by that one performance. The Mayor presented me with an address and a diamond star inscribed, "Presented to Miss Geneviève Ward by her grateful friends in Melbourne, November 6, 1885." The idea for this presentation had been sixpenny subscriptions, not to exceed five shillings in any one case; and I believe it was started by the servants at Government House. They raised so much that, instead of only an illuminated address as was intended, they had enough over for the star.

Now came the question how to get the rest of the money. It was the law, or the custom having the force of law, in Australia at that time—I do not know if it obtains now—that when any charity benefit was raised in this way the Government should give an equal sum. Sir George Verdon took me to see the Premier—the same one who had let me keep my little dog—a nice man, and I claimed £2,680. He seemed aghast.

"Impossible, Miss Ward."

"Is it not the law?"

"That may be, but all the charities we have had to deal with have amounted to ten or twenty pounds net for the proceeds—a great deal of the money taken having gone in expenses and luxuries, carriages, suppers and so forth."

"Well, I have managed better than others, so I claim £2,680."

Both Sides of the Curtain

He finally yielded, and with £5,860 thus realised the ward was built and named after me.

They wanted me to give another performance of *Antigone*, but I refused. I was very tired with all my extra exertions for the performance, and I said it should be my last in Melbourne, which it was.

Sir George Verdon had a very beautiful place in the country, next to the Governor's on Mount Macedon, about thirty miles from Melbourne and 8,000 feet above the sea. It was called Alton. He had brought every tree from England, as in Australia there is only the eucalyptus, of which there are three sorts, the blue, the red and the white. The eucalyptus does not shed its leaves, it sheds its bark. The effect of the white trees by night, when the bark is shed, is beautiful and weird. They suggest ghosts.

Sir George Verdon invited me to spend a couple of weeks there to recuperate, and I had a most delightful time. The Governor and his family were charming neighbours. Sir George, who was a fine elocutionist, read the " Rubáiyát " and " The Light of Asia " to us.

A curious feature of the plan of his house was that each room formed a separate building under a separate roof. The drawing-room was a marvel —large enough to contain a full-sized organ, and all panelled in New Zealand wood. The roofs, too, were most artistic. It was the show place in Australia. They had a beautiful billiard-room as well. A very charming lady—Mrs. Orr, the widow

The Other Half

of a General—came up to stay with me because there was no lady of the house.

I went back to Melbourne, and after staying a few weeks there we took steamer to Sydney.

During my Australian trip I had a very interesting experience with a young girl. She was the daughter of a miner from Ararat, and was a schoolteacher of Scottish descent. Her name was Nelly Veitch. She had come to Melbourne with the idea of giving recitals, and Lady Lock and the Bishop's wife were much interested in her, and asked me if I would take her on tour with me when I went to New Zealand. I told them that my company was fully made up, but if she would like to come simply on the chance of doing something and understudying, I would give her a modest salary to start with and pay her fares. We started, and Mr. Vernon took a great deal of trouble with her, rehearsing her in all the different parts which she could understudy, and she was a very apt pupil. When we were in Wellington the lady who played Queen Anne, Mrs. Foley in *Forget-me-not*, and other middle-aged parts began to put on airs, and, instead of keeping to her part when other dialogue was going on, she would chatter and disturb the performance. Mr. Vernon, as stage-manager and an autocrat in that function, called a rehearsal specially to bring her into line with the rest of the company. She refused to attend. He sent her back a message that if she did not she would not play again. She again refused, and he said to Miss Veitch, "Could you play Queen Anne to-night?"

Both Sides of the Curtain

She was terribly frightened, but said she would try. There was no trouble about dressing her, as the costumes were mine. She played it without a hitch, really better than the other lady, who, unfortunately for herself, thought she had us in a cleft stick, as it was impossible to get any sort of actress in New Zealand. Miss Veitch remained with me, playing different parts, until I left Australia. Then she applied for an engagement at the Theatre Royal, Melbourne, where they were doing a pantomime or something of that kind; but what she saw was so different from what she had seen with us that she determined not to continue her career as an actress. So she took up teaching, and did so well that she earned a thousand a year. She is a great teacher of elocution and of physical culture, for she went into that too. In a new and thriving country almost any kind of aptitude counts.

I left Melbourne on November 25 and arrived at Sydney on the 27th. While I was at Sydney waiting for the steamer I visited the Blue Mountains. They derive their name from the blue gum trees that clothe their sides. There is wonderful railway engineering between them and Sydney. The line then ended at Oberon—a city of twelve houses. We drove from there sixteen miles in a buggy, and walked two and a half miles down the mountain to see the stalactite caves, the Imperial Cave and the Devil's Coach House. Some of the stalactites are exceedingly beautiful. One looked like the statue of a young girl; some of them like lace-work. It was a glorious trip.

The Other Half

We returned to Sydney, and I left Australia December 1, 1885, in the steamship *Australia*—our captain was Captain Brough, a cousin of Lionel Brough of the famous theatrical family. The steamer was very unseaworthy; I think it was her last journey. There had been a terrific storm, but the curious thing about the Pacific is that after a storm the sea begins almost immediately to make a delusive promise of living up to its name and, with a difference, is like glass. For the change does not preclude a ground swell in which you go down, down, down, and then up, up, up. Everything on the steamer was tied with string or rope. I called it "the stringed ship." Captain Brough never expected to reach land. We were even tied into our berths. It was the most uncomfortable journey I have ever made.

However, we arrived at Honolulu, the capital of the Sandwich Islands, on December 17. In those days the islands were ruled by a king—Kalikoa. Honolulu is very beautiful; you look down from the ship into the sea and see the coral at the bottom, it is so clear. And then, perhaps, in front of you, or over you, you have a magnificent rainbow. There is very seldom any rain, but sometimes from a beautifully clear blue sky, without a cloud and with the sun shining brightly, there will fall a shower, so to say, from nowhere. The island on which Honolulu stands is partitioned by a mountain, and we went up this mountain on horseback—the women even riding astride, but not in trousers, only in a sort of sheet wound downwards from the waist. When

we got to the Pali, just on the highest point near
the top, we had to leave our horses and crawl up
on hands and knees: the wind always has things
its own way there.

The King and Queen wore European dress. The
women, what they call a *holucu*, a thing made exactly like a nightgown with a yoke. A stout lady
so attired is a sight in a gale.

Next to Colombo it is the hottest place I was
ever at; the thermometer is 88 all the time.

The Royal army consisted of a very good band,
one general and half a dozen soldiers—not quite
enough for the " wars that make ambition virtue."

I saw the jail with its 165 inmates. When we
arrived the priest was saying mass, and after the service the prisoners eat their *poi*—a sort of paste made
of a huge vegetable as big as a man's head and like
a potato. This is crushed in tubs and left to ferment.
I tasted it once, and, alas! can almost taste it yet.
It suggested something from a bill-poster's can. It
is the general food of the natives, that and raw fish,
octopus and shrimps; they pull the heads off the latter
and eat them forthwith. The Chinese came there
years ago and brought one of their terrible maladies
—leprosy. I went to a leper settlement where they
made researches into the disease. Some children
were housed in two separate buildings with no direct
communication between them. In one they were fed
on European food, in the other on the native diet.
It would be interesting to know the result; at the
time of my visit they could not tell precisely how
the disease was contracted. They had given prisoners

condemned to death the alternative of inoculation for purposes of experiment. One man there at the time had submitted to this to save his life. He remained perfectly well afterwards, yet they were going to inoculate him again. So it was capital punishment after all, only with aggravations of sheer brutality. If he had had the pluck to sue in the courts he would have won his freedom—though perhaps he might still have wanted the luck to find a second Portia for counsel. The hospital was a range of wooden houses opening on a veranda. In one of these we saw an auction taking place: a dying leper was selling his few clothes to his companions—a nice way of earning assets for your last will and testament. There was one poor leprous woman whose head was like an enormous potato; you could not distinguish her eyes or nose or anything, and the comparison ran to colour as well as to shape, for they are a dark people. Her husband was so devoted to her that he had taken the position of attendant in the compound. The sisters in charge of the sufferers show the greatest devotion; they do everything for them as they would for other patients, and some of them contract the disease. But they won't allow visitors to touch anything that has been handled by a leper, not even the pen with which one writes one's name.

As we went along—it was New Year's Day—the poor creatures would hide, then rush forward to wish the matron "A Happy New Year." It was quite heartrending.

Here it was that my little Thekla fell out of my maid's arms and broke her jaw. She was then

eleven years old, and there was only one horse
" vet." in the place. He could do nothing for her.
I asked him to show me how the bones knit together.
He said there was a sort of jelly that exuded, which
hardened and became harder than bone. So I made
linen muzzles for her, and she kept these on all the
time, and was fed with a teaspoon. For one month
she never left my maid's arms or mine. The little
thing was so clever that after a time she knew she
must not scratch off the muzzle, and she would sit
up on her hind legs to be fed. We all had our
reward when, finally, we were able to take the
muzzle off and found the bone had set. There was
but one drawback—the nursing balked me of a
visit to the Lake of Fire. For all that, I was lucky
enough to get sight of what looked like a sea of
fire as the waters glowed in the intense light of
the sun. With my stage training I was easily able
to take it as an excellent substitute for the real
thing.

We had the honour of visiting the King and
Queen, who expressed a desire to have us play
Forget-me-not. Well, there were only myself and
Mr. Vernon of the cast of the play. Fortunately,
it is very small and requires only six persons. There
happened to be in the hotel Mrs. Strong, step-
daughter of Stevenson, with a niece of Hollingshead.
One was married to an officer there, so, with their
aid and that of an American newspaper corre-
spondent and an English gentleman, we were able
to get up a performance. We played at the pretty
little theatre, or rather hall, and it went very well.

The Other Half

Our audience included the American Minister and many of the missionary families.

In Honolulu a debtor is not allowed to leave the island, and one of our company was in that condition. This seems a strange way of paying old debts, to compel the defaulters to contract new ones; in fact, to throw good money after bad.

I left Honolulu on February 14, 1886. The journey to San Francisco was a trying one, it was so very stormy. On our arrival at the Golden Gate it was impossible to cross the bar, which is there three miles wide. I think we were as many days outside before the pilot could take us in. The waves were so high that the hatches were battened down, but the captain allowed Mr. Vernon and myself to share the bridge with him. It was a gorgeous sight—the great bar, with the waves rushing over and every seventh wave about twice the size of the others. The only difficulty was to start in time to dodge the bigger one. However, the pilot did it. If one of those fine fellows had caught us we should have been swamped; and where would have been my world tour then? Our first excursion on landing was to Monterey, one of the most beautiful places in California. Some of the old mission houses are very interesting, and the coast and the drives all round Monterey are beautiful, and there is a wonderful hotel in magnificent grounds.

The day I arrived in San Francisco, at the great Palace Hotel, a card was brought to me, "Aunt Corda is waiting for you," with the number of her room. I think I frightened the waiter, for I jumped up and ran. The writer was like a second mother to me, though she was not even my aunt. She was the widow of Colonel Milton H. Sanforth, a great sportsman who used to run horses for the Derby. It appears that she was in New York when she received my letter saying that I should probably be in San Francisco at a certain time. This was enough; she took ship, rounded South America by Cape Horn, and all on the mere chance of a meeting. It was the most exquisite surprise I ever had in my life. I loved her as I loved my own mother. We remained in San Francisco a short time—about a month—and on April 1 Aunt Corda decided that we must have a holiday.

We left there at 4 P.M. for the Yosemite—Aunt Corda, her companion, Mr. Vernon and myself. We arrived at Barenda at six in the morning, breakfasted, and went on twenty miles to where the railroad ends. The coaches had not come from the Yosemite to meet us, and we remained all day in the Pullman, eating our meals from the basket which the manager of the hotel had kindly provided for us. The other passengers did not fare so well. At 7 P.M. the coaches came, and we were sent back with the returning passengers to Barenda. We were fortunate in getting one room for the three of us—Aunt Corda, myself and the companion—at the little inn; Mr. Vernon slept as best he could in the hall. The other passengers were eight or ten in a room. The next morning the coaches were ready for us (the railway has now superseded them). We drove till three, when we lunched at Grant's

Hotel in the mountains, then rested two hours and went higher and higher still, in snow up to our axle-trees. The moonlight effect of the whitened landscape was lovely. All the morning our route had been through the most glorious hills and valleys, glowing with wild flowers of every colour, purple and yellow predominating. We arrived at Clash's at 9.80 P.M.

The next day we were called at five, and started at eight in a small coach and four. The lunch basket came in useful, for we changed horses only at the top of the mountain. The snow had an exquisite effect on the giant pines. There is one with a hewn arch wide enough to take a coach and six, and with a branch six feet in diameter.

A poor Chinaman in the coach with us, who was looking for a berth as a waiter, had but his little cotton jacket on his back, so I gave him a blanket, for which he said, " Muchee thankee. Muchee faree?" in the pidgin-English which once led a compatriot of his to say of an electric car mounting a steep ascent: "No pushee, no pullee; goee like hellee!"

On reaching the Yosemite Valley we spent the afternoon washing the mud off our clothes and wraps, as it had rained and snowed all day. The hotel at this summit is not suitable for wintry weather. After dinner we went to the tree parlour, a detached room built around a mighty tree 86 feet in circumference. We munched pine nuts round a blazing fire of logs four or five feet long and with a great old-fashioned chimney six feet wide. Next morning we walked to the foot of the valley, deep in snow, and drove to the Mirror Lake to see the sun rise over the giant cliffs. In the afternoon we had an exquisite drive to the cascade at the other end. Next day the grandest sight I ever beheld opened out on reaching Inspiration Point. No words can describe the beauty of the background of the valley of El Capitan, facing you—8,000 feet of rock, straight, perpendicular, with 900 feet of waterfall in The Bridal Veil, the most beautiful of many others of its kind.

On leaving the valley we came to the most primitive of all houses and warmed ourselves. Fortunately, we had brought our lunch with us, though the others managed with ham and eggs cooked by the teamsters. We went on and arrived at Clarke's at four, and started at ten next day for the big trees. The snow was very heavy, and we could not get to the upper groves. The trees grow large so gradually that one does not realise their size until the Grizzly Giant is reached. We rested under its shade and returned at 8.80. We had to wait for the coaches and were very cross. We walked out and found a curious snow flower which looks like a red asparagus; birds, deer, foxes and squirrels abound.

We left at last. All the party from the Yosemite arrived, and we mustered a big crowd. We arrived at Grant's at eleven, after a tough pull over bogs of mud, in which we got stuck once and had to get out in order to relieve the horses. Judge Grant, a millionaire, ran this hotel in the middle of the wilderness.

The Other Half

On my return to San Francisco I was quite ill with concussion of the brain from a fall from the ladder of the coach, and I slept for several days. Thanks to this remedy, I managed to play *Forget-me-not*, *Guy Mannering*, and *The Queen's Favourite*, and I made arrangements with the manager for a return tour to America in the following year.

We left on April 25 for New York. There are a good many routes from San Francisco, but we took the Rock Island line, by the snow-covered sierras. You hardly realise the ascent, as the gradients are so very gentle. After changing cars at Ogden we passed into the desert, a great desolate waste. On reaching the summit, at 8,200 feet above the sea, the air was so rarefied it was difficult to breathe. At the top there is a curious monument to Oakes Ames, who was so largely interested in the building of the Union Pacific line. We came out of the desert through Echo Cañon and Weber Cañon, by the Devil's Slide and Pulpit Rock. Now it was no longer still life, but thousands of prairie dogs in their burrows, and cowboys in dug-outs. We arrived at Omaha on the 28th in rain and snow, and crossed the Missouri and changed cars at Conal Bluff. The trees were budding, as it was early spring—the first time I had seen them for three years. We arrived at Chicago on the 80th. On the 81st we got up early to see Niagara and dined at Syracuse; from Albany we came down the lovely Hudson shore.

We left New York May 15 and arrived at Liverpool May 26. So ended our tour of the world.

CHAPTER IX

TEACHING FOR THE STAGE

SHORTLY, after my return from the tour of the world in 1886, I took part in a sort of experiment in high drama that interested me almost as much as anything in my whole career. We played Tennyson's *Becket*, then called *Fair Rosamund*, at Canizaro Woods, Mr. Schuster's place. It was but a sort of trial performance, which had to wait for years to mature in production on the stage. The great man was present at the rehearsal—he did not face the performance. It was very windy, and I had to exert my lungs to be heard; so, though we gave it but three times, that was quite enough in the circumstances. The open air is a great trial for the voice if the wind blows away from the audience. The Prince and Princess of Wales were of the party, with some French royalties and many of our Royal circle, as it was for a charity. The diction of the piece was exquisite; its dramatic capabilities left much to be desired. For all that, I think it is too generally assumed that the one precludes the other. It does not in Shakespeare, nor even on the French stage. *L'Aventurière* is a good acting play as well as a well-written one. The plays of the younger Dumas are better even to read than to see; half the time the characters are sitting at their ease for a chat, as though "resting" after much exercise with the limbs in pieces of "action." The British demand for constant exercise, even in drama, while blameless, is purely local, like the taste for Norfolk dumplings with good boiled beef. "Cut the cackle and come to the 'osses" is hardly to be made a canon of art. What splendid talkee-talkee there is in *Ædipus*, *Antigone* and *Medea*.

Tennyson was most enthusiastic about my Queen Elinor, and I think he there and then made up his mind that the part should be mine if ever it reached the stage. Certain it is that my subsequent performance of it, with Irving, was due to an expressed wish on the author's part.

Our Canizaro play wanted but a more southerly summer to make it a bit of the dreamland of the golden age. An amateur, Lady Archibald Campbell, who got up the performance, belonged to the brilliant circle under the leadership of Jimmy Whistler, then at the height of his social and artistic fame. But it was good to see their gambols in the joy of life. With the setting of the woods, it suggested a certain historic garden of Florence in the olden time, where they told the stories that made the *Decameron*.

Very different, in all but the text, was Irving's version of the acting play, prepared for the production of 1893. The piece underwent an extraordinary change, for it had been severely "pulled about" to make it suitable for the stage. The

words were all the poet's, but the sequence and the
disposition were wholly the actor's. A critic of the
time drew up a laboured comparison between them.
It was not free from errors of fact, but it is still
useful as showing the fundamental difference between
the barely poetic and the acting drama. Walter
Map, a sort of English Rabelais, dropped out of the
cast. The five acts were condensed into four. The
prologue remained, but its order was changed; the
curtain rose on Elinor and Fitzurse in a Norman
castle, not on Henry and Becket. Act I., which
in the poem is extremely long, was clipped of the
whole of Scene IV., in which the great archbishop,
finding that his lordly guests come not as bidden to
his banquet, sends out into the highways and by-
ways and invites the halt and the maimed to his
board. So that, later, when the four knights enter
with murderous intent, the beggars, with their
"crutches and itches, and leprosies and ulcers, and
gangrenes and running sores," drive them off in
terror of contagion, and thus cover Becket's retreat
to France. It is a fine scene in the tragedy, but, as
a critic said at the time, it was a whiff too pungent
for any sort of attempt at realisation. Act II. was
in one scene, passed in Rosamund's Bower, and compounded of the first scene of this same act and the
first scene of another, a condensation wholly com-
mendable, however viewed. Act III. opened with
the meeting of Louis of France and Henry of England, and from Louis's lips we had the only fresh
lines written for the stage version, explanatory, time-
saving words. Scenes II. and III., the most mag-

AS QUEEN ELINOR IN "BECKET."

nificently dramatic passages Tennyson ever wrote, were passed in and outside Rosamund's Bower, and culminated in the intensely thrilling moment when Elinor's dagger, as it grazed Rosamund's white bosom, was arrested by the sudden steel clip of the archbishop's hand. Melodrama furnishes no situation more breathlessly sensational, more unexpected. Here we had to regret the loss of a strong interchange between Elinor and Fitzurse, but still in favour of the dramatic concentration. So in this, as in every other case, we saw the essential difference between an acting and a literary play. Again and again, what the poet was obliged to describe Mr. Irving had to act. The latter crystallised words into action; descriptions became deeds. Take another example. When Becket, early in the play, threatened to smite Fitzurse with his crozier, we missed the line—

"'Fore God I am a mightier man than thou;"

And yet we did not miss it, since it was realised in the towering muscular spirituality of Irving's " mitred Hercules."

Acts III., IV. and V. were telescoped. We saw Henry in his Norman castle, and Becket rating prelates and barons. Elinor rushed in, adding to the monarch's fury against Becket, while Henry uttered the historic cry :

"No man to love me, honour me, obey me.
Will no man free me from this turbulent priest ? "

Scenes II. and III. showed us Becket in the Augustine monastery of Canterbury, with faithful

Both Sides of the Curtain

John of Salisbury imploring him in vain to fly his doom; and the destined victim, in the great cathedral, standing before the altar, gigantic, epic, great of faith and defiant strength, challenged and welcomed martyrdom. While the mailed murderers did their work thunder growled forth the wrath of Heaven, lightnings flashed through the church as they fled, and Rosamund, penitent and sad, crept from the gloom in which she had been telling her beads and knelt beside her strange protector, the slaughtered saint. The political matter concerning the young prince had been wisely cut away. Elsewhere we traced the touch of Mr. Irving's blue pencil, deleting here lines and half-lines, intensifying the dramatic significance at all times, pruning the strong phrase of Tennyson—especially in the mouths of Fitzurse and Elinor—to the squeamish ears of a London audience.

We had a revival of *Becket* on July 9, 1894, for two weeks, and then toured with Irving from September 17 to December 18, I still as Queen Elinor.

A very interesting event in 1898 was our playing *Becket* at Windsor before Queen Victoria and the Royal Family on March 18. Taking a company down to Windsor, though a great advertisement, is a very costly one. The theatre at the Castle being very small, our manager had to have new scenery painted, and with this to take down all the *personnel* of the theatre, stage hands, electricians, etc., as well as the company. All for one night! We had a special train, and on our arrival at Windsor in the morning rehearsed on a small stage in St. George's Hall. Irving, Ellen Terry and myself were given sitting-rooms in which beds had been placed for us that we might rest before the performance. Mine was the Holbein room, and it was a delightful experience to rest surrounded by such glorious works of art. Queen Victoria evidently enjoyed the performance, for she led the applause. I remember how startled I was to hear great approval of passages of secondary importance that would not have got a hand in London.

After the performance Irving, Ellen Terry, Terriss, and myself were presented to the Queen. I was astonished to see how very short she was, especially by contrast with her Indian attendants. She was most gracious, and I was impressed by the beauty of her voice.

I shall never forget an incident when I was playing in *Becket* at the Lyceum. Mr. Gladstone came to the back of the stage during the performance and sat in the O.P. entrance, where an armchair had been placed for him, with a heavy curtain behind it to protect him from the draught. He talked to me during an interval between the acts. His share of the conversation, if such it is to be called, was one long series of questions about America, its life, its cities, its people. Every few minutes he kept saying that he wanted to go there, it interested him so much, and sighing because it was impossible, as he had so many things on his hands at home.

So it seems to come to this: drama is an art

for players quite as much as for writers. Both have
to learn their business, and when they have done
that the stage will not fail to do its part as a teacher
for the general community. In my own department
of it I owed much to others and at least as much
to myself. For the final word, of course, is, " Think
for yourself."

In 1890 I commenced coaching for the stage.
My system was to teach pupils to trust to themselves.
I did not " parrot " the girls by merely showing
them how to do a thing and making them repeat
it; I urged them to give me their own sense of a
character or a situation by discussing the piece with
them, and particularly all that bore on their own
part. Very often when we came to a phrase they
did not understand, I would put it into ordinary
language to enable them to seize the meaning in that
way and to give the proper inflections, which then,
of course, they could apply in the language of the
author.

Another thing I was very particular about was
the emission of the voice. I always sent them to a
singing teacher, not to learn how to sing but to
learn how to breathe. Many breathe with a closed
throat, and too audibly to my taste. I did not
teach that branch myself because it is rather tedious,
although any good singing teacher can, in a dozen
lessons, cure this practice of producing uncalled-for
sighs.

Another point was sending them to learn deportment. For this they went to Madame Cavalezzi,
who taught them dancing as well, with the result of

graceful carriage and no awkwardness with hands or feet. It was a different type of dancing then, and a great deal was toe dancing. The greatest stage dancers of a still earlier day were Taglioni, Cerito, Grisi—not the singer, of course. In my time, as a singer, at the Scala and other great opera houses the ballets were not merely entertainments, but regular plays without words, sometimes acted in pantomime by *mimas*, or mimics, who rendered their parts by gesture and facial expression. Some of these performers were also dancers. The ballet was a great trial for the regular vocal artists, because it was placed near the middle intervals of the opera, and lasted about an hour. The consequence was that the singers had to wait, and their voices, as it were, cooled, to say nothing of the break in concentration on the general movement of the piece. Madame Cavallezzi was a great *mima*. I saw her in two pieces done in that way—*Mephisto* and *Monte Cristo*—at the Empire, and she was superb. She married one of the Maplesons. I missed her very much when she went to New York, where she is now the head of the Academy of Music, teaching the ballet. She was a great help to me with my pupils, for gesture and deportment.

Dancers lead a trying life; they have to practise incessantly, like the pianists. A day's intermission and the limbs might cease to be lissom; a good dancer is almost dislocated from childhood. They have to begin very young, and all the great ones have started in their pupilage as quite little children. In Italy and France there are Government dancing academies, where every care is taken of them.

Both Sides of the Curtain

Regular appearances on the real stage form part of their training. At the Academy in Milan—a very fine one—they are driven to and from the Scala in special omnibuses.

Dancing fifty years ago was much more of an art than it is now, though there has been an improvement of late, and we have had fine dancers from Russia and Italy who are really trained, among them Lydia Kyasht. The discipline is almost military. I fancy they pay but little for their training, as the better-to-do do not, as a rule, let their children follow this career. The Conservatoire of Paris is not run for money, but for the glory of art. The English are too independent for all that.

Among my pupils in pure drama was the daughter of my old friend Antoinette Sterling, Jean Sterling Mackinlay. I trained her entirely; she was with me a year. At first I thought she would be a tragic actress, for she had quite a deep voice for a girl, and at school used to write Roman tragedies and play in them. But her voice changed, and comedy claimed her for its own. When I considered her fully prepared I took her to Benson and asked him to give her the privilege of walking on with his pupils and starting later with small parts, so that she might get accustomed to stage work from the beginning. He kindly consented, though she was not a pupil of his, and she took her first steps on the stage at the Comedy in his production of *Coriolanus*, when I played Volumnia for the first time in London. Benson's method, I think, is the best of all, to judge by the number of stars of the stage who have passed through his hands. His constant change of parts and constant rehearsals is a great advantage; his school gives practice as well as precept, and in every branch—dancing, fencing, and all that pertains to the stage. He keeps his pupils in fine physical training with games, hockey and cricket and everything of that sort; and, as they advance in proficiency, he starts a company of them for smaller towns and gives them the principal parts. I never saw a man more popular with a company; he is so courteous and kind in every way. Highly educated persons come to him for their stage training; the men are mostly from the colleges. Such a pupil makes a more finished actor, though an uneducated one may have more magnetism. The latter, however, is in the nature of a gift.

My appearance with him in *Coriolanus*, at Manchester, led to a series of our joint performances at Stratford-on-Avon in the Memorial week, and at other places, and also to a friendship that will last as long as we do. It has been, perhaps, the most interesting experience of my theatrical career to be associated with such a perfect artist in his great work of familiarising Shakespeare with the present generation. He has lifted the mind of the people to a realisation of the greatness of the greatest dramatist of all ages, and has spent in his great and patriotic labours time, talent, and fortune, in a generous giving of self which I have never seen equalled. He has been ably and devotedly seconded in some parts of his work by his wife, especially in the dancing and designing dresses. We have, alas! for the period of the war lost their services to the profession. Sir Frank and Lady Benson have long been at the front, where their valuable work for the comfort of the soldiers at the canteen under their charge is greatly appreciated. Their customers in this humble calling are counted by the thousand.

When I had been teaching some years Mr. Vernon joined me, and we made a sort of academy of it. He had been teaching for over fifty years, for he was stage-manager, as well as actor, at the Theatre Royal, Bristol, under Chute's management, then the hot-house of histrionic talent for the whole country. In that capacity he taught almost all the actors their parts, and once Grundy said to him, during a rehearsal of *The Queen's Favourite*, " Ah, Vernon, I wish you could play every character in the piece! " Whereupon I made him my best curtsy and said, " Thank you! " Vernon could not only say that a thing wanted doing, he could show how it was to be done. I mostly taught the tragedy and he the comedy—he was a perfect comedian.

I often refused pupils and kept girls off the stage, for it is a very hard profession anyway, even when you can hope for success; and when you cannot it is heart-breaking. I sometimes had to be cruel to be kind, and to nerve myself to send some applicants away in tears to save them from greater anguish to come. A lady came to me quite lately, a very handsome woman, who had been on the musical comedy stage, and I asked her to recite something. She said she knew nothing. I gave her the trial speech of Queen Katharine, explained the situation, and even recited it for her. She returned in a week and rattled it off as a child might "Mary Had a Little Lamb" at a school treat. I then told her that I saw no glimmer of dramatic instinct in her rendering of it; and as she said she could get plenty of concert work, I advised her strongly to go on with that and give up any idea of the stage. In spite of this, she asked me if I could give her a letter to Sir George Alexander. What could I reply but, "I never give letters to managers unless I consider the bearer has some vocation for the career."

"Oh, but you can give me that," she said.

This was a little too much. "I can no more give you vocation than I can give you a nose if God has not provided you with that at the start. I can only train you in the use of your powers."

Another of my pupils, a wealthy woman, after a few lessons quietly offered me a hundred pounds for an introduction to the same eminent manager. I told her this was not my line of business. She then, quite unabashed, asked for a letter to another manager of a far different stamp who had just produced a piece which I knew to be a failure. The very mention of his name made me feel full of mischief—for reasons. So, still waiving my fee, I undertook to inform him that she wished to appear at his theatre in a walk-on.

He loftily assured me that he engaged only players of experience.

"It does not matter," I said coldly. "The

lady is an heiress to millions, and she will no doubt easily find what she wants elsewhere.''

He at once changed his tone. ''Send her to me and I will see what I can do.''

As I expected, it was not long before he offered her the rights of his derelict piece for the provinces for £2,000, with his aid in the production, and this on the very eve of its withdrawal! I then told her what I knew about it, and she, of course, declined.

I thus cried '' quits '' with the manager in question, who, in my earlier career, had tried to play me an equally dishonourable trick.

Revenge *is* toothsome, if you don't carry the taste for it too far.

I had a rather funny letter once from a butler in some castle in Scotland: he wished to join my company, as he felt he could act, and especially women's parts! Need I say I declined the honour?

I have, as I say, kept many young people from the stage because I thought it was a duty to save them from needless disappointment. Two very charming girls sought my aid, but I refused it because I saw they had no asset but prettiness. However, they got engaged to walk on in *A Midsummer Night's Dream*. At the dress rehearsal they were given an Amazon's costume with tights. They were very modest girls, and they said to me, ''Don't you think if they put us at the very back of the stage we might do it.''

I sympathised with them for reasons I have given elsewhere, but I was obliged to say : '' Unless you hold a position that gives you the power to refuse you will have to go wherever you are told, even if it is in the front row.''

They gave up the stage, and I honoured them for their grit. I have had many letters from girls whom I have, so to speak, warned off. Many have said : "Oh, but I want to *do* something.''

"Go and help poor women in the slums.''

One girl listened to me and started a refuge for street women. She saved a great many, and afterwards wrote to thank me, for she had found the work of her life.

A very nice girl, with quite a pretty talent, when she had finished her studies with me, put it before her family that she wanted to go on the stage. She wrote me quite a heart-broken letter to say that they—rather important, not to say self-important, people in the Midlands—absolutely refused to give their consent, as no woman on the stage could be respectable. I asked her kindly to tell them, with my compliments, that the average of self-respecting women on the stage was quite as high as in society, and that a woman who wanted to go wrong would never lack opportunity, and a woman who didn't would never take it. I then cited many names of actresses, well known and unknown, whose lives were as pure as any woman's could be—good wives and mothers and all pertaining. I added that, unfortunately, the limelight gave notoriety to the bad ones, and so the profession was judged by the acts of a few.

As to the teaching, personally I am in favour of a provincial novitiate, preceded, perhaps, by a walk-on or two, in some of our leading London theatres. The last named is a study in itself in facing the footlights and in getting accustomed to the sight of an audience. A sharp girl will pick up a great deal in watching others, and need never fear she is losing time by playing subordinate parts in a first-class company. It is the greatest mistake to try to rush a London audience with raw material. A good provincial tour is a sovereign remedy for amateurishness. I can hardly impress strongly enough on beginners, and especially on the good-looking ones, that they should never be above starting in a small way. Nothing is more fatal to success than conceit; the most beautiful actress living may do herself lasting injury by trading solely on the attractions of her face and form. A boom will do something for a time, it is true, but it cannot carry the matter through.

Judging by my own pupils, I should say that there is a very fair field for *real* comedy (a rare qualification nowadays) and a practically poor one for tragedy. The demand does not set in this direction at the present moment, and, in any case, tragedians are few and far to find. As for other branches of the art, such as the dramatic, for instance, I think that some excellent work is being done, and that plenty of half-blown talent awaits the call.

It is very much a matter of fashion. When I first came to England, after years of success in opera, with my proud repertory of well-known tragedies for the stage, I could not get even a hearing. One manager actually offered me a singing part in a burlesque. When at last an engagement came, it was only effected at the cost of the entire proceeds paid in advance into my agent's hands.

The tragic gift is more rare, for the obvious reason that tragedy involves both physical and moral strain. The outward and visible must be there, as well as the inward and spiritual. Tragic lines of feature and form and a tragic voice mean half the battle, but these are not always to be found in combination with the requisite temperament. Jewesses and people of southern race have sometimes this in the blood, but, as a rule, there is very little real inborn tragedy. The sheer power of will counts for something. When I first played in Manchester I knew I was not going to fail, because I had made up my mind on that point. I felt that I was going to strike twelve, but I did not know it would be so loudly. You see, I had realised that I had no time to fail. I did not make my appearance on the theatrical stage until I was six-and-thirty. What was to be done had to be done quickly. My heart was in my work, and the character of Lady Macbeth was one to which I had given long study. A concatenation of circumstances helped me, as it nearly always does. I was able to study the sleep-walking scene from life, for two children whom I knew had the habit of talking and walking in their sleep. The voice issues quite differently from sleepers, and the breathing is very laboured. Then, again, a person who walks in sleep does so with wide open, unblinking eyes; I never closed my eyes during the sleep-walking scene, but the strain was dreadful, and they were bloodshot after the performance.

I look upon the character of Lady Macbeth as a most engrossing one, and one which is also very clear for study. She is an ideal wife, her every thought is for her husband's advancement; she has lost her children, and all her love has gone out to her husband; she is ever loyal to him, she never upbraids him but when he wavers in his purpose of ambition. The sleep-walking scene is the murder in an awful retrospection which she is powerless to resist. Awake, she lives in the present; asleep, her will loses its control of impressions, and remorse does its work in spite of her. Without doubt she dies from the effect of conscience, claiming its own the more mercilessly for her attempts at repression. It robs her of her rest, and so the line, "You lack the season of all nature, sleep," carries a double meaning. Yes, but when sleep has itself been "unseasoned" for its task!

At the time I am speaking of, the Manchester audience was an extremely critical one. It had been educated in Shakespeare by Charles Calvert, the successor of the younger Kean in Shakespearean production, so the favour it showed me—and it was great—was something of which to be really proud. Later, as I have said, when I played Lady Macbeth in Paris, I acted it in French until I came to the sleep-walking scene, but, by Regnier's special request, I played this in English lest the public should refuse to believe that I was not of French birth. I shall never forget that performance, and I think there are still many who could say the same thing. During the scene I threw my hands backwards, as though to shake the blood from them, just after the words, " Will these hands ne'er be clean? " A long shuddering sigh accompanied the action and passed from the stage to the audience, who, in that moment, became absolutely one with me. What shall I say of it?—it was my exceeding great reward.

One of the greatest of the changes in the profession, to my mind, is in the status of the supernumeraries. I remember that when I came to London in '75 the Adelphi super was not exactly convincing as a person in society. He was addicted to baggy trousers and cotton gloves in ballroom scenes, and as for his womankind—well, the sole excuse for them was Mrs. Poyser's : " God A'mighty made 'em to match the men." Now, at the St. James's, for instance, the extra ladies and gentlemen are mostly used to their parts in real life, and want no teaching in manners and customs.

CHAPTER X

PLENTY OF EXERCISE

I MADE an American tour from September 21, 1886, to April, 1887, then came back to England for an autumn tour of the provinces, and followed this, after a break, with tours in 1888-89. So one way or other I had no lack of exercise during the period named.

I opened on September 26, 1886, in New York with *Forget-me-not*. During my stay there we had a lovely trip up the Hudson river, passing the glorious Palisades to West Point. The trip was organised by a friend on his yacht, and the ten guests or so were to be entirely invited by me. Of course, we visited the great Military Academy at West Point. We were royally entertained there by the staff, and had a most delightful return by the incomparable Hudson.

Next it was Montreal, Ottawa, and back to Massachusetts. Then we had a series of terrible one-night towns—Springfield, Worcester, Providence, Rhode Island, Lowell, Portland, &c. After that Baltimore for a week, Philadelphia, and another series of small towns in the Southern States. At Delaware we found a charming theatre, but had to dress under the stage, within range of the stench

Plenty of Exercise

from a cesspool—such is the Southern carelessness.
We made a sharp protest about it—such is the
Northern fuss. At Wilmington—I think it was—
our hotel was at the top of a hill and the station
at the bottom. On our leaving, in icy weather, the
horses could not manage the descent, so we took
arms and slid down the whole way.

The one-night towns were very trying. Sometimes we travelled three and four hours from one
town to another in hot cars that would have baked
pork and beans. It was a lesson in stoic endurance.
An Indian might have quailed under it without a
murmur from the tribe. We played each night and
went on next morning under much the same conditions. Once in a way might not have mattered,
but six times a week! Then there was the mode
of travelling; unless you had a cabin—and there
was only one on each car—it was more than horrible, as it often is to-day on the sleeping cars for
the longer journeys. There are two sets of beds
one above the other, and these run all but the
whole length of the car. Each has its single lodger,
man or woman, with nothing between them and the
Age of Innocence but a scrap of curtain in front.
You wake up in the morning, if you have slept
in that stifling atmosphere, and you look out to see
a man's legs protruding from out of the curtains—
maybe a fat German's! I tried it once, never again!
If I could not get a cabin I sat up all night, a
blessing in disguise, perhaps, for it gave me a chance
with the scanty supply of water for the toilette. I
met Pullman once, the inventor of these torture

chambers, and gave him a piece of my mind. "Why not,' I said, "sleeping cars for women and sleeping cars for men, in separate compartments? Ladies and growing girls should be spared such trials." He had nothing to answer: in fact, I never gave him a chance. I refused to go to America with Irving, when he took *Becket*, because he could not guarantee me a sleeping-car. The only time when the Pullmans are really luxuries is in the day hours—when their sleeping accommodation is not in use.

In the Southern States the travelling was very slow. On the small lines they had negro firemen and engine-drivers. We quite often found the train stopped in the middle of a plain and the excited passengers putting their heads out to inquire what was the matter, only to be informed that fireman or driver lived there and had gone to give a look in on his family. I have known them to pull up for short conversations on the way. Mind, I am speaking of 1886; I don't know what it is now.

These trials were bad enough for us who had learned fortitude by years on the road. What must they have been for those who had to bear them for the first time?

A British friend of mine has obligingly given me this aspect of the question. Think of the academic recluse who has been induced to try his luck with a message to mankind in a lecturing tour! A Matthew Arnold, for instance, or a second Emerson. Pitchforked red-hot into a cold town for one performance, with an early call for next morning

Plenty of Exercise

for some remote part of the planet where the next is due. Dickens, they say, was killed by that second American tour, though he was a hardy annual if ever there was one. I am thinking, says my friend, of the "feelosofer" from Oxford, England, or from Cambridge, Mass., who has but one thing to say, and has come blinking out of his cell to the Lecture Bureau to get it said. His business, perhaps, is to tell you that nothing matters in this earthly pilgrimage if only you keep cool and live by the priceless precept of the Japs: "Avoid anger, worry, hurry, and fear." "Keep cool," with that stove going till he frizzles in his oven like St. Lawrence on his gridiron! "Anger," while the demon boy scours through the cars and chucks literature at you for sale or return, with no care in his aim! "Worry," and all the rest of it—while the whole principle is to deny you for one single moment the possession of your own soul! Fancy having to walk almost straight from such an environment to an improving discourse on sweetness and light, exemplified in your platform manner! A doctrine that could come victor out of that would conquer the world. The most exquisite scene in Molière is the breakdown of all M. Jourdain's professors of the art and wisdom of life under far inferior trials. They are so piteously sincere, but they can't stand the conditions. The American academic comes nearest to the harmony between precept and practice. My friend was much edified by the *manner* of a lecture by Henry Ward Beecher. The great man appeared to the minute and, laying his watch on the table, began to the second. When his hour was up he fobbed the watch again, and with a curt bow vanished so quickly that he almost led the procession on the way home to supper. The moral for others is—if you retail wisdom from a tub, stick to it till your customers come to you.

In January, 1887, we started at Brooklyn and went on to Toronto and Cleveland. I stayed there with my cousin, Belden Seymour, one of the old residents. He gave a reception in my honour to about two hundred people, and among them I met a very old American actor, Murdocke, an interesting relic of the past. At St. Louis I stayed with my old friends the Newton Cranes. Newton Crane is now the only American barrister practising in London, and he is attached in that character to the American Embassy. I visited Louisville, Indianapolis, and St. Paul, Minnesota, now virtually one with Minneapolis. The Mississippi at Minneapolis is bridged; and this is more than you can say of that mighty river in every part of its course. I had a delightful time tobogganing. A great feature in these places is the building in winter, with blocks of ice, of large castles and statues before many of the shops. The ice is shaped with red-hot knives. The cold is so persistent that these things last for months, and are quite an ornament to the city. The same practice prevails at Montreal. One can go into the wonderful ice castles, but cannot linger long there, the cold is so intense. I have never felt the cold so piercingly as I did at Niagara Falls, when the ice below the falls was forty feet deep in the river. The wind cut the face as with knives, and icicles hung from men's beards and noses. We went on the ice, clambered over the rocky boulders, and saw the falls from below—a wonderful sight. Luckily, we found a little log-house where they sold hot coffee. When we returned to the hotel to straighten our bonnets or hoods, I think I had the surprise of my life—my skin was absolutely canary-coloured, where it was not a rich purple on the cheeks, and I had a temporary jaundice from which I thankfully recovered in the course of the day.

From St. Paul we went back to Chicago, where we remained a fortnight. The Palmer House refused to take me in on account of my pet dog, so I went to Leyland's, which did just as well. What is too good for my little dog is not good enough for me. This was one of the few places where they refused hospitality to my inseparable companion. Monterey was another. On leaving Monterey the conductor told me I could not keep her with me, and she must go in the baggage wagon. I said, "All right," and took her there, but was not allowed to share her captivity. "Have it your own way, but we go together; love me, love my dog." Whereupon they relented, and, on my promise to keep her quiet, we both returned to the car.

I visited the Board of Trade while I was in Chicago. It was very little better than going into the monkey-house at the Zoo; in fact, no better, except that there was no disagreeable odour; the men seemed quite wild, and danced about like the monkey tribe.

Both Sides of the Curtain

My next visit was to Milwaukee, the saddest incident of my journey, for I went to see my father's grave, where he had lain for eight years. Then some more short journeys and one-night stands. We reached Calamazoo at 7 P.M., were personally conducted in a large omnibus to the theatre, played there, and, after the performance, returned to the station, where we could get nothing to eat but bread and cheese or "pie." There we waited for the train till 12.30, and our next stages were London (Ontario) and Hamilton, where I stayed the night with some dear old friends of my childhood, the Ridleys, who had settled there. I left at seven in the morning and went on to Boston by Niagara and Syracuse, arriving at Boston at 9 A.M. next day, tired out. I had a very pleasant surprise at the Brunswick Hotel, where my rooms had been decorated most charmingly by my old friend Miss Lilian Whiting, the poetess. Everything possible had been done for my comfort—writing materials, sewing materials; and even Pond's extract for my eyes, in case they were tired, had been thought of.

Then again for one-night stands to Brockton and to Salem—where our esteemed ancestors used to burn their witches—Chelsea, Taunton, Fall River and Newport. These were the most tiring parts of the tour. We finished up with a week at New York, then took ship for England, and after my return I visited Paris in May.

I began my next English tour at Plymouth, and we were there on June 20, 1887, Queen Victoria's first Jubilee Day, when the whole kingdom

Plenty of Exercise

seemed ablaze with bonfires. I wanted the manager to close the theatre, but he refused, and I played *Forget-me-not* to the enormous sum of £8 5s. We then went to Torquay for three nights. Our next journey was rather curious, for we travelled on three different lines and changed cars four times to get to Weymouth. One would hardly have thought there was room enough on the island for so many twists and turns. Next came beautiful Guernsey, where we played a week and took a lovely drive to St. Oban where the Comte de Paris was in residence. We were received by the Duc de la Tremouille, who courteously informed us that ladies were not admitted. No wonder they never made his master king of the French! However, we got over it by visiting a very old church, A.D. 1111. Our days were spent in such drives, one especially to La Grêve du Lac lingers in my memory. Our audiences were charming, and our manager, Mr. Rousby, made everything comfortable for us. We came, at Portsmouth, to a very different state of things—what we call a "nut-cracker" audience. Some members of the gallery thought it might be amusing to pelt me with the refuse in shells and orange peel. Whereupon Mr. Vernon, one of the gentlest of men, was roused to violent anger and, addressing them without the customary "Ladies and Gentlemen," threatened to stop the performance at once if it happened again. After that they were as quiet as whipped curs. It was the first and last offering of that kind in my whole public career, and I am bound to say I prefer wreaths.

Both Sides of the Curtain

During my stay there we visited the old *Victory*, Nelson's flagship at Trafalgar, and the beautiful *Osborne*, the Royal yacht. Her commander was one of the staff that came over with me from South Africa. The tour ended in June.

In August we began another tour: Brighton, Hull, York, Newcastle, Edinburgh, Dundee, and Glasgow. We crossed to Ireland by the route from Stranraer to Larne, the worst Channel trip I ever made; everybody on board was sick, even my little dog. Fortunately, it is a very short crossing. On our return we took Liverpool and then Manchester, where Emily Faithfull gave a large reception for me to about one hundred and fifty people, among them the two Misses Gaskell and Miss Hope Glyn. Whilst in Manchester I also had the delight of meeting again the Bishop and Mrs. Moorhouse, whose friendship in Melbourne had been very precious to me. I lunched with them and spent a charming afternoon at the Episcopal Palace. The Bishop was very fond of Thekla, as of all animals. He had brought from Australia a little quadruped, not a bear but like one, which he was trying to acclimatise.

We went on to Sheffield, where the smallpox was raging, and for a week we never saw the sun or blue sky. I need scarcely say that business was not booming. Leeds, Birmingham, Nottingham, Cardiff followed, and at the last-named town we visited the beautiful Llandaff Cathedral, and ended the tour in Bristol on December 17.

In my well-nigh unfailing experience all audiences are interesting and appreciative in their several ways. My dear Irish audiences seem to take you as a personal friend. The difference between them and the Scotch is most marked. In the latter case you may have to wait long for the verdict, but when it is given you may be pretty sure it will not be reversed. As for the foolish saying that they have no sense of humour, I do not know any people with more of it. The English are more prone to enthusiasm in the theatre than in private life; with the French it is the other way. A Manchester audience is perhaps the most critical of all.

In 1888 I went on tour again, beginning in January at Worcester, and at Coventry making the customary pilgrimage to the window of Peeping Tom; then by Leamington, Southampton, Hanley, Chester and Southport to Blackburn, where I met Emily Faithfull's nephew, Bishop Cramer-Roberts, by whom I was charmingly entertained. In the course of conversation I asked him why the children's death rate in Blackburn was so much higher than elsewhere. Was it the buildings? "No; it is because our factory mothers, many of them girls, go to work in the morning and leave their babies without care, food or attention." He was doing his best to remedy the evil, but it was very uphill work. I went on to Manchester, where I found my dear old friend Miss Emily Faithfull ill; then to Leicester, and on returning to London played a week at the Lyceum in *Forget-me-not*. I also produced *The Lodestone*, by W. H. Vernon and T. Edgar Robertson, at a matinée, but I dropped it, as it proved no lodestone for me. I had the same ill-fortune in the following year, 1889, with my production at the Grand Theatre, Islington, of *Forgotten*, by Frankfort Moore. Its title was the prophecy of its fate. There was a better omen in that of *Forget-me-not*.

The remainder of 1888 was passed in resting, and in a visit from my dear Aunt Corda, who came from America and stayed wth me from June to December.

It was still plenty of exercise in the years that immediately followed from 1890 to 1894. I have already dealt with one form of it in my account of teaching for the stage, which I began in 1890, and which was active life of a kind, though it was all done at home. And for more of that life, in the ordinary acceptation of travel and actual bodily movement, there was the great South African tour to be dealt with in my next. This alone, it will be seen, took up the better part of a year between 1891-92. I resumed coaching on my return in 1898. I played Elinor in Irving's great production of *Becket* at the Lyceum, followed by a long provincial tour—also dealt with in detail elsewhere. In 1895 I was again engaged by Irving to play the part of Morgan Le Fay in the *King Arthur* of Comyns Carr. Ellen Terry was not strong enough to play more than six times a week, so, if there was a matinée, Irving played another piece at night in which she was not wanted. In all we played *King Arthur* a hundred times.

My next engagement with Irving was in 1896, when I played the Queen in *Cymbeline* from September 22 to December 11, and rehearsed *Richard III.* In this, for the first time, I played Queen Margaret of Anjou. The part of Margaret has generally been cut down, but Irving restored the text for me. The last rehearsals were very trying, as they took place after the night's performance, and we sometimes went on till two, three, and four in the morning. Irving never spared himself or anybody else.

On the first night of *Richard*, December 19, 1896, after a very great success, Irving, on returning home, fell on the stairs and injured himself. Of course, for the time being, this stopped the run, and as it was not a slight injury it was decided to continue *Cymbeline*, with an understudy for Irving's part. When he got better we resumed *Richard III.*, and it was played from February 27 to April 7, 1897. In May of the same year I played Mrs. Borkman in Ibsen's *John Gabriel Borkman*, at the Strand Theatre for a week. In 1898 I appeared with Ellen Terry at the Fulham Theatre in *Othello*, playing Emilia to her Desdemona. In February, 1899, I played Volumnia, again with Benson at Glasgow.

The next part I created was at the Adelphi in Norman Forbes's production *The Man with the Iron Mask*, in which I played the part of Queen Anne of Austria from March to May, 1899. A curious thing about that part was that though I was only ten minutes on the stage it was one of my greatest successes. This shows it is not the length of a part, but the grip of it that tells. The queen is an old woman dying of cancer in great agony; and there is something epic in the conflict between the strength of her spirit and the weakness of her pain-racked frame.

In 1900 I was still coaching, and I continued to do so from time to time till I gave it up for good in 1905. In the interval, 1902, I played the Marquise in *Caste*, at the Haymarket, with Cyril Maude and Miss Emery.

In October, 1906, I was the blind queen in *The Virgin Goddess*, by Rudolf Besier, under the management of Mr. Otho Stuart—the most genial of managers. The play had but a month's run, though it deserved a greater success, for it was finely written and superbly mounted. The great thing in it was the blind woman. There were only two scenes, but they were magnificent. They would have been very trying to the eyes if it had been a long run; in the second act I stood for twenty minutes facing the audience with a glassy, unbroken stare. This gave the appearance of blindness. My eyes ran water after and ached badly for a long time. When I was a child my brother and I used often to see who could look the longest at the other without blinking. When first I played Lady Macbeth I thought the same device would give me a look of being asleep, and I went through the whole scene without moving an eyelid or even as much as turning the pupil. As I turned, the eyes went with the head. In this way, when I came to play in *The Virgin Goddess*, I knew how to get my effect, and, although the strain was twice as long as that of the

Photo: L. Caswall Smith.

AS THE BLIND QUEEN IN "THE VIRGIN GODDESS."

sleep-walking scene, I was able to do it. It was the greatest physical trial I ever had. In women's parts, as a rule, there is no great physical effort required, though that of Queen Katharine demands a terrible expenditure of nervous energy in the death scene. Among men's parts I should think Macbeth is one of the most trying in this way, though other tragedies, particularly Othello, run it hard.

A long part, again, is usually trying by its length, apart from any exceptional calls on the strength of the actor. In *Forget-me-not* I was hardly off for a moment, and when I did escape it was only to change the whole of my costume; so there was no rest. A comedy part may be very heavy also, if you are on the stage the whole time, because you have to keep your spirits at the proper pitch. Ristori would rarely play more than three times a week; she said no one could be " great " oftener than that. But it is not the custom in France or Italy to play tragedies eight or nine times. In England she had to play six times, but she used to be terribly exhausted; I have seen her go to sleep while taking refreshment after the play. In an important part we give out our vitality until the whole system is lowered, and then 'ware colds, or anything of that sort there is to catch. Many in the profession, instead of going straight home from the theatre and getting to bed, indulge in clubs, hot suppers, all-night bridge or other foolish devices for turning night into day. Anyone who takes an art seriously may be content to live for that alone. This rule has stood me in good stead, for now, though within a few weeks of eighty-one. I am able to do work as hard as many women less than half my age. Naturally, in this homily I have not in view the people that play in musical comedies, reviews, and that sort of thing.

In April, 1907, I played *Coriolanus* with Benson at Stratford-on-Avon. I shall never forget my arrival in the drenching rain that Sunday morning; yet we started for a walk through the soaking fields to Anne Hathaway's cottage—a distance of five miles. I have also in my memory a sight of Clopton, where Shakespeare got the idea of the manner of Ophelia's death. We went also to the celebration at the church, and Marie Bremer sang beautifully.

On November 80, 1908, there was a memorial performance at His Majesty's for Ristori, and I think every actor and actress of importance in London played. Personally, I did the sleep-walking scene, with Mr. Fisher White as the physician, and Miss de Silva (Mrs. Martin Harvey) as the gentlewoman. I also read the beautiful Ode written by Louis N. Parker. The proceeds formed part of a fund to erect a monument to Ristori's memory in her native village.

I now began to think that I had earned a holiday, so, in the spring of 1909, when my pupil, Miss Veitch, visited England, we took a trip together to Holland. We arrived at the Hook on May 2 at five in the morning, and put up at the Hotel Pauley, then " did " the House in the Woods for the paintings by Rubens, and the Museum for the Rembrandts, all in one day. " Quite American," some will say. " Let them say on "—pure surface impressions are the gems of travel for that vast majority to whom it is all new. So I make no excuse for telling you that at Delft the canals run through the streets with perfectly charming effect. At Amsterdam, as faithful students of our guide books, we failed in no *devoir* to the Rijks Museum. Nor did we neglect the Queen's Palace, where they have a marvellous ballroom 100 feet high, if you please, 160 long and 60 wide. Think of that, with a good partner, the court orchestra, and the " Blue Danube " " in play," and who would not be young again? The valse is hackneyed, I know, and the Danube is not always blue. A lot of it is grey, but we all come to that; it is a very old river. We returned constantly to the Rijks Museum for the Rembrandts, and Ruysdaels, and the Gerard Dows. Then we saw the diamond-cutters at work. It is very easy to get about Amsterdam, for it abounds in electric trams, all numbered, so you have no trouble in finding the way. We visited many small places, among them Middelburg, in Zeeland, one of the most interesting old towns. You see a great many Spanish types there. After the long struggle for independence many of the Spanish remained as settlers, and, incidentally, to preserve their national manners, customs and beliefs. It is curious to notice the difference in dress between the Catholic and Protestant women. The Protestants wear no jewellery, the Catholics are gorgeous in gold head-bands and necklaces of garnets, rows deep. Their men even are wonderful in silver buttons and buckles and things on their clothes.

There is a beech tree at the hotel in Middelburg which is said to be the largest in the world—though, of course, I should be glad to stand corrected from the United States. If that's impossible we must order one at once; I await with hope, not unmingled with—well, never mind!

At Marken, one of the little islands in the Zuider Zee, the girls and boys are dressed alike until they are six years old; the only distinguishing mark is a little round patch on the caps of one sex. At eight they cut the boys' hair, and at sixteen the girls', at the back, leaving only two side curls for the face. Marken is like a village of opera bouffe. In Zeeland the scenery is very different from that of the rest of the country. They have English hedges, and red roofs to the houses, and the roads are bordered by trees. In the upper part of Holland the canals and windmills are most picturesque; the fields are tiny islands encircled by canals; you have often to cross a bridge to enter the houses. Big dogs are harnessed to little carts; what would Thekla have thought!

The tulip fields are one of the most beautiful sights. A special narrow-gauge railway goes right through, and on both sides there are fields of tulips and hyacinths—acres and acres, and each field with its own colour.

From Leyden, after a two hours' run to Haarlem, you revel in the glory of Franz Hals.

Plenty of Exercise

There is a very interesting cheese market at Alkmaar, and they have quaint weighing-machines. The men who carry the little cannon-balls of food on trays often stagger beneath their burden. These market porters are all dressed alike, with the exception of their hats of different colours, according to the Guild—green, yellow, red and blue.

I did enjoy that outing!

CHAPTER XI

MY SOUTH AFRICAN TOUR

I LEFT England on November 25, 1891, under the management of Luscombe Searelle, who took a company out to support Mr. Vernon and myself.

We had a most delightful journey to Cape Town, though not an idle one, for we rehearsed several of our plays during the voyage, the captain having marked out a part of the deck, which was covered in sail-cloth, for *our* mimic of Shakespeare's "mimic stage." It was very different from Atlantic travel; once at Madeira the weather was warm, and we wore muslin dresses and practically lived on deck, trying to keep cool.

Charming entertainments were got up on the steamer—a smoking concert in the fore part of the deck and a fancy dress ball and concert in the saloon. The captain lent Mr. Vernon his uniform for the ball, and everybody said the new wearer looked his part more than the owner himself.

We arrived in Cape Town on December 8, and opened on December 10 in *Forget-me-not* at Exhibition Building, a most extraordinary place. We played ten pieces in four weeks.

Cape Town is most interesting for its dominating Table Mountain, usually covered with what they call

My South African Tour

"the Tablecloth," a cloud that hovers and hangs down over it. The south wind is the cold one there, and is called "the Cape Doctor," as owing in part to the mixture of different breeds, natives and Indians, etc., it is not a very healthy place, and would be uninhabitable but for the breeze from the mountain.

December is in their warm season, so it is difficult to eat your plum pudding with conviction on their Christmas Day—to say nothing of the dessert. I counted seventeen varieties of fresh-grown fruit at table one day : the Kafirs revel in the open street in what in England would be the costliest dainties of this kind. I had the good fortune to find there Sir Henry and Lady Lock—this made it ever so pleasant for me.

We left Cape Town on January 9, 1892, and arrived at Kimberley on the 11th. The journey is very beautiful going through the Karroo desert. The scenery is lovely : you see whole fields of arum lilies and all kinds of coloured flowers, masses of them, hedges of geraniums and wonderful white roses, with snow-clad mountains to close the view. Kimberley is a very uninteresting, flat place in the middle of the veldt. Almost the only attraction is its wonderful diamond mines and the curious big hole, as deep as a large house is high—I forget how wide—which marks the spot where they dug out the first diamonds before the machinery came. We played there four weeks. I found that the chief engineer of the De Beers mine, Louis Seymour, was a distant cousin of mine, and that his wife was also connected through another branch of the family. This made an additional attraction for me.

While there, Mr. Vernon was stricken with Cape fever, and when his son told me I sent him some aconite. I was the company's doctor always. My master in medicine was the greatest of our homœopathic physicians—Dr. Garth Wilkinson, who for seventeen years kept my brother alive—and thus I learned a good deal. Mr. Vernon recovered in three days, to everyone's amazement, and played on the fourth night. Still, my patient had called in the first practitioner in Kimberley, much to my annoyance. When I reproached him for this, he said he had done it because, if anything had happened to him, I might have got into trouble; but he had taken my physic only, and not the doctor's. The latter's reputation was immensely enhanced by this marvellous cure, as it generally took weeks to get over an attack. We left it at that.

From Kimberley we went to Bloemfontein on February 8, and played there one week. Then we started for Johannesburg. At that time there was no railway between the two places, though it was in course of construction. So we travelled in a Concord coach, which is an American invention and, with its C springs, very comfortable. The route was frightfully dusty, and we were soon all converted into granite statues in appearance. We had twelve horses and two negro drivers. One held the reins, the other the whip, but this creature often jumped down and ran forward to flog the leaders. Very cruel: I had quarrels with him. We were

My South African Tour

three days on the road. Starting at four in the morning, we reached our destination at the next stand at midnight, getting wretched meals at little hotels on the way. We slept as best we could in the four hours that remained. One night my bed was a bag of potatoes, there being no other accommodation—*and I slept!* We arrived in Johannesburg pretty tired. The town had very curious contrasts, no pavement of any kind, yet the streets lighted by electricity, and the place but five years old.

There were no roads between Bloemfontein and Johannesburg, but the traffic made its own tracks. When one got too bad for further use they made another by its side. As you travel over the veldt you see nothing like a tree except one specimen of a kind of monstrous bush—the Wachteenbeetje—in English the "Wait-a-Bit." Its thorns are two inches long, and the sheep find it easier to get into these bushes than to get out.

There was a nice theatre and a fair hotel at Johannesburg. My rooms were peculiar. The state room was just large enough for a table for four people, in the centre, with sofa and chairs round. The bedroom, on the contrary, was very large and magnificently furnished—and why? Because they were Barnato's rooms, and he was in England at the time. The rats were again a pest, as in Australia, and they had not far to walk to business, for I was on the ground floor. One night there were two in my room. I summoned the night-porter and made him take me upstairs, where I had less splendour but a bed to myself.

Both Sides of the Curtain

We played in Johannesburg eleven weeks and produced sixteen plays. The work was very hard, as we had a change of bill every three nights, and we had prepared only some ten pieces on our starting for Africa. We had soon to put more in rehearsal. Our success was so marked that we even gave six of Shakespeare's plays, till then a thing unknown there—*Macbeth, Othello, Hamlet, Merry Wives of Windsor, Merchant of Venice,* and *Much Ado About Nothing.* New scenery had to be found for every play, and it was painted on calico. Then there were the costumes which I had to supervise not only for Othello and Hamlet, but for Falstaff and Rob Roy. The Fat Knight especially was a terrible trial, and Rob Roy was no joke. Our company was not large enough for the Shakespeare plays with many characters, and we had to get local assistance, which, thanks to Mr. Vernon's wonderful stage management and coaching, did very well.

While I was there I also had my share of illness. I was struck down with influenza the first night of *Much Ado About Nothing.* I wore two fur coats in the wings, while everyone else was melting with the heat, yet I shivered during the whole performance. I went back to the hotel and told my maid to give me aconite, keep me well covered, and on no account allow anyone to come in. There was quite an excitement in the town, as in a small place like that everybody knows everybody else's business, and, besides, the people were especially interested in theatrical matters. The work went on just the same, for Mr. Vernon stepped in with his great play of *Mammon*, in which my part could be played by an understudy. In three days I was up and doing again. The manager of the theatre, the manager of the hotel, and all the people I knew in the town had come to beg me to see a doctor, but I would not. Dr. Wilkinson was with me in spirit, I am sure. A few days after my recovery I met a medical man on horseback. He jumped off, introduced himself, and said : " Miss Ward, will you tell me why you would not have a doctor? "

I replied, " For the simple reason that his business would have been to keep me in bed as long as he could, and mine was to get up as soon as I could."

We left on May 15 by coach, but this time only for a journey of five and a half hours to Pretoria. The first view is very beautiful. You may call it a garden city surrounded by hills. The air is the most balmy I ever experienced. There was one very imposing structure, the Government House, which seemed totally out of place in what was otherwise almost a village. Kruger lived in a sort of bungalow with a veranda all round it. I went to the Government House to see one of our consuls and was afterwards shown into the Strangers' Gallery. There was a sort of state chair for Kruger in the centre of the hall, while the other members were ranged in wings beyond, each with a glass of water in front of his seat. We waited for a few minutes for the great man, and he arrived in a shabby old coat that might have served as the only covering for a *sans culotte*. The first thing he did was to use the back of his hand as a pocket-handkerchief, then he opened his cavernous mouth in a gargantuan yawn, whereupon, fearing that I might fall into the cavern, I fled.

The streets outside were watered by three convicts under a guard with pistols, and they deluged the road with a hose on wheels. The theatre was a small building, because the Boers do not patronise that institution. The curtain was a most extraordinary one, painted on canvas with oil paints, and depicting, I think, Venus rising out of the waves. It was difficult to see which was Venus and which were the waves. The auditorium was also a pigeon roost and, of course, very dirty. However, we played there four weeks.

There is a very curious big tree outside the town, and I went to see it. An old Boer was sitting on the ground with his back to his house, and I asked him the way. He shook his head and said, "Yo-no." The hatred of the Boer to the English was then very marked. Knowing this, I said, "American," whereupon he relaxed and said, "Yee-er," pointing in the direction where the tree stood. It certainly was an extraordinary growth. The branches, when they got to a certain length, dropped towards the ground and took root on their own account. The whole thing was very old and of an enormous extent, capable of sheltering two thousand people. I also visited the Crocodile River, very beautiful, and running through a narrow, long valley surrounded by hills. We stayed there a day or two at a little farm-house. Returning, I saw one

of the most magnificent storms on the veldt at night.
The lightning illuminated the whole horizon. We
were told that often a team of sixteen bullocks, eight
a side, and held to the centre rope by chains, were
struck by the lightning on one side and all killed,
while those on the other remained unhurt.

When we left Pretoria one of our company had
bought a tiger. The poor thing had been orginally
injured in some way when it was a cub, and had
been in a family for a long time. However, our
comrade thought he might turn an honest penny by
making a show of it in Johannesburg. It was accordingly packed in a large hen coop and sent with
the luggage in an ox cart, which started several
hours before us. When we overtook the cart we
heard that the tiger had escaped. Somehow we all
felt most sorry for the half-tame wild beast. We
saw nothing of it on the way, but when we got to
Johannesburg we raised the hue and cry for it by
telegram, and in two days had a reply: " Tiger
found—forwarding it! "

Large game of that kind are rare in this region,
though some traveller has talked of meeting a drove
of lions. As a matter of fact, they do not go in
droves at all—only in families, father, mother and
cubs. I was asked by an interviewer if I had ever
met one. I rose to the occasion. " Yes," I said,
" I was reading one day on the bank of a stream,
and I looked up and saw a lion just across. I had
heard of the power of the human eye over animals,
and I fixed the lion with my gaze and looked steadily
at him. My attention was distracted for a moment

and I looked away—I heard a noise—I looked back."

"The lion had gone?" said the interviewer.

"No," I returned softly, "he was dead!"

We arrived in Johannesburg June 5 and played there two weeks. During the run of *Hamlet* occurred one of our tragedies in real life—I am sorry to say there were two. Miss Josephine St. Ange, a charming actress, formerly with Irving's company as understudy for Ellen Terry's Ophelia, was playing that part with us. She was driving with a woman whom I had warned her against as not knowing the tail of a horse from the head. On the veldt the horse ran away, the driver was thrown out, while Miss St. Ange lost her presence of mind, leapt and fell on her head. A gentleman who had witnessed the accident rushed up, found her bleeding from the nose and ears, and sent a Kafir to the hotel with a note for me. I have that note still. It is scrawled in pencil on a leaf torn from a pocket-book, and thus it runs: "Miss Ward, Grand National Hotel. A lady whom I take to be Miss St. Ange, though not sure, has been thrown out of a trap and is lying insensible in a house near Auckland Park Hotel. Bring a doctor at once.—S. MacColl."

It roused me from my afternoon rest, and I at once took a cart and, guided by the Kafir, started for the scene. The people of the house were away; I found Miss St. Ange on the ground, quite unconscious, and in the care of a Kafir servant and the writer of the note, both quite dazed. They had not even taken off her gloves or her shoes. It was nearly time for me to be at the theatre, so I asked Mr. MacColl if he would take her to the hospital. He at once consented, and we improvised a rude stretcher, carried by four Kafirs led by himself with a lantern. It was one of the saddest sights, that little procession wending its way over the veldt to the hospital. The people there at first refused to receive her because she was dead, for the poor thing had succumbed on the way, but they were induced to put her in the mortuary.

Meantime we had gone to the theatre and begun *Hamlet* with an understudy. After the first act the manager came to us with the fatal news, and we at once dismissed the audience and did not play again for two days. In Johannesburg burial had to take place within twenty-four hours of death. We all went to see our comrade and pay our last respects at the grave.

A slab of white Sicilian marble, with this inscription, marks the spot where she lies:

MISS JOSEPHINE ST. ANGE

(MRS. FELL)

BORN MAY 28, 1845; DIED JUNE 9, 1892.

In June we made a tour to Pietermaritzburg. From there we went to see the hut of a Kafir chief named Tetclekas. It was like all the huts, made of a sort of twisted bamboo covered with grass, and entered by a door about two feet high. The floor looked like polished black marble, but in reality it was made of cow dung which the women press out with their feet and stamp on until it becomes as hard as marble. The Kafirs sleep on this floor, with curious little wooden benches as pillows that fit into the neck. The only furniture was a set of false teeth that hung up in a little bag. The chief was not there himself, but there were about a dozen of his wives to do the honours. One, a very old woman, got quite into a rage with me because I had a veil on, and insisted on my taking it off. Then the children entertained us with a weird dance. The Kafirs do not repudiate their old wives, even for temper, but simply add new ones at need. I fancy my hostess on this occasion was on her way to the retired list.

Durban, our next town, was sheltered by fine hills covered with pineapples. It had a good hotel and there was a charming drive up the hill into some lovely woods, where the people live in summer. We took steamer from there to East London, also on the coast. The river there is very fine, and we were taken to a picnic on its banks. Our route was lined by multitudes of monkeys jabbering and chattering—monkey scandal, I dare say. The flowers were beautiful—one, the aphobia, was yellow, blue and red in colour, a perfect Joseph's coat.

We played there, then went on to King William's Town and Queenstown, and returning to Johannesburg on August 2, played four weeks.

On August 23 came our second tragedy. Mr. Eyre, our juvenile lead, died within a few days of disease of the lungs. His death was caused, in my opinion, by the awful dust. As I have said, there were no pavements even in the market place, where the oxen lay all the winter long in a foot of mud. This dried in the summer and caused death-giving dust, which affected the stomach as well as the lungs. I never went out without a silk handkerchief tied over mouth and nose, and I strongly advised my company to do the same. I have known the dust so thick in a moderately wide street that you could not see the houses opposite. It is the African substitute for London fog.

Mr. Eyre died in the evening and was buried the next morning—he had already turned black with decomposition. We all went to the funeral, and when the body was carried from the hearse to the grave we had to give brandy to the bearers.

All this so frightened the company that they went to Mr. Searelle and said they would not stay till the end of the season. We accordingly left on August 81 and arrived at Kimberley on September 8. Of course, we still had to go by the coach to Bloemfontein. An exhibition was going on at Kimberley, and when we arrived the Governor and his family were there. Cecil Rhodes was there too, and this made it very pleasant. Rhodes was a very absent-minded man. He went to the exhibition one day without any money in his pocket and when they refused to let him in, he said: "Why, I am Cecil Rhodes!" "That may be," was the reply, "but our orders are to let no one in that doesn't pay." Rhodes was obliged to borrow his entrance fee from a friend who was passing. He was also a very nervous, sensitive man. We went to lunch one day with the Governor, Sir Henry Lock, and Rhodes did not appear. We waited I should think about fifteen minutes, and Sir Henry said to me, "What shall we do?" I replied, "Why, in my little way I never wait more than ten minutes for anyone." "No more will we," he said, and in we went. When we were about half through Rhodes appeared. His explanation was that he had to review some troops as colonel, his first appearance in that capacity, and he had had so much trouble with his uniform that he could hardly get it on or off.

We played in all, in South Africa, twenty-six plays in nine months. Here they are: *Forget-me-not, Mammon, The Queen's Favourite, A Scrap of Paper, Married Life, Guy Mannering, Nance Oldfield, Last Word, Still Waters Run Deep, Peg Woffington, Macbeth, London Assurance, The Two Orphans, Much Ado About Nothing, Rob Roy, Lucrezia Borgia, Hamlet, The Merchant of Venice, Snowball, Othello, The Merry Wives of Windsor, Pillars of Society, Jim the Penman, Married Life, Bess,* and *Last Legs.* I never worked so hard in my life. We practically lived in the theatre, rehearsing from 10 to 8, and playing at nights. Fortunately there were no matinées. We left Kimberley on September 19, and had a very charming journey owing to the companionship of an Archdeacon and his wife, not of the same tribe as the Bishop's wife in Christchurch.

Our audiences were most appreciative, and the local Press, while preserving perfect freedom of judgment, was both guide and friend. The public interest in the plays was most stimulating to the actors; our coming was always the event of the day in the town. Hard measure was sometimes dealt out to the local supernumeraries, but probably it was all taken in good part. The *Johannesburg Star* clamoured for *Macbeth*, and got it. "The management," it said, "should finally decide to put on *Macbeth*—which it is very eagerly hoped they will see their way to do. For the sake of seeing Miss Ward as Lady Macbeth, we would forgive the inevitable supers; and Birnam Wood might come to Dunsinane in the paws of a score of painful greenhorns and cream-faced loons, if we were only permitted to see Miss Ward as tragedy queen. A foretaste of her powers we have had in *Forget-me-not*."

Mr. Vernon was equally well received for his performance in *Still Waters*. "Strong, complete, rounded, lifelike—adjectives fail to convey one's admiration of the perfect art with which Mr. Vernon portrays the part of John Mildmay, who saves his domestic happiness by prompt, keen, decided action, with a blunt, matter-of-fact exterior which covers the tenderness of the loving husband. The whole interpretation is consistent; and Mr. Vernon has never so thoroughly demonstrated his complete command of manner where the spoken words alone would be only half the battle. It is true artistic insight to have perceived that the dramatic intensity of the scene with Hawksley, in which he unveils his knowledge of the polished villain's past career, is sufficiently obvious to the most ordinary playgoer not

to require exaggerated emphasis. The highest resources of his art are employed in bringing out in
full relief the delicate features of the less-obviously
dramatic situation with the woman whose reputation
he has saved—partly for her own sake, and also
partly with a view to the restoration of domestic
peace and concord. Mr. Vernon's was indeed a
thoroughly splendid performance throughout; in
comedy his equal has never been seen in Johannesburg.''

On the 21st we lunched at Government House,
Cape Town. Admiral Nicholson and his staff were
there, and we bade farewell to Sir Henry and his
lovely wife. The admiral and ourselves were fellow-
passengers on the journey home, and I need not say
we had a delightful time. I beat them all at whist.

We arrived at Plymouth on October 9, 1892, and
here endeth the second lesson, or shall we say the
South African trip?

CHAPTER XII

NEW SCHOOLS FOR OLD

THE talk about new schools of drama as final things is almost as silly as the talk about hats in the same connection. There is but one eternal thing in all art—and especially in this one—the something strong, simple and natural in character and situation without over refinement in conception and, above all, without any tricks of mood or manner. At one period artificiality prevails, then that artificiality is the second "nature" to which it is the actor's business to work. You must be true to your conventions, for they are the working realities of every age.

For me I always think in terms of persons, and persons are ever the same with merely a difference of setting. There is always a Garrick, actual or potential, always a Kemble, a Siddons, a Rachel, a Macready, or a Kean. I am obliged to think most of the Ristori of my time, because she was nearest to me in sight and touch—that is all. If I happened to encounter her as Mrs. Siddons it would have been just the same. She was one of my earliest recollections of the stage. My mother took me to see her very often in Florence when I was fifteen. She had not then been out of Italy, but her reputation there was enormous. Her leading man was Rossi, a fine actor. She was born at Cividale del Friuli in 1822, and both her parents were on the stage. At twelve she played the parts of pages and small servants, at fourteen and a half she created the part of Francesca da Rimini. Later on she married into one of the great Roman families, and became the Marchesa del Grillo. In 1850 she retired from the stage, but returned in 1853, and in 1855 made her appearance in Paris and at many cities in France, at Brussels, at Berlin, and then returned to Italy, in 1856 and 1857, to play in her native land. Later on she went to Vienna, Paris, London, Berlin, Warsaw, then toured the United States, and in South America. On returning to Europe she was seen in Denmark, Switzerland, Norway. There was hardly a large town on the Continent where she had not appeared. In fact, she saw the whole world of her time, and the world saw her.

In 1882 she commenced representations in English as Lady Macbeth and Mary Stuart. In 1884 she had a magnificent benefit in Paris, and then played in America—in English. In 1885 she retired again—this time all but for good. Strange to say, her farewell performance was in New York, and in English, at the Italia Theatre, with German actors, for the benefit of the German colony, and with a translation of Schiller's *Marie Stuart* for the piece— a perfect hotch-potch of play, players, languages, and what not, if ever there was one! And even this was not all, for she revisited the glimpses of the scenic moon for a charity performance as Lady Mac-

beth, with Rossi in support. A commemoration
ceremony in his honour brought her to Rome again
in 1896 to declaim the fifth canto of Dante's *Inferno*
—think of that again for the majesty of her rendering of it! And still not for the last time. She had
to repeat it in 1898, at the opening of the Great Exhibition in Turin. In Paris they wanted her to take
the place of Rachel at the Théâtre Français, but
she refused, owing to the difficulty of rising to her
own exacting standard of the management of the
French idiom. So Legouvé partially compounded
the matter by persuading her to play *Medea* in
Italian, Rachel having refused the part as "unnatural." It accordingly became one of the finest
gems of the Ristori repertoire.

It was my privilege to teach her the English of
Lady Macbeth and Mary Stuart. She found difficulty with the pronunciation, and the word
"murky" especially troubled her. "*La vostra in-
fernale lingua!*"—your infernal language—she
used to say. She was quite right. Why have we
knocked off, as with a hammer, all the terminal
vowels of elision that made the music of our tongue
in Chaucer's time? What a triumph for some of us
who manage to get some music into it still! But,
oh, the horror of it, when consonant meets consonant
in the tug of war.

Dear Ellen Terry, in her "Story of My Life,"
makes fine fun of the struggle of the old Kemble
school for their lost vowels. Irving attends a reading by Fanny Kemble, and in his own words,
"After a portentous wait, on swept a lady with an

extraordinarily flashing eye, a masculine and muscular stride. Pounding the book with terrific energy, as if she wished to knock the stuffing out of it, she announced in thrilling tones :

> "' Ham-a-lette,
> By
> Will-y-am Shak-es-peare.' "

And so on. To be fair, the attack was in the nature of a retort provoked by Fanny's assurance to the effect that she had never seen any of the modern school in Shakespeare, and thought that she "should find such an exhibition extremely curious as well as entertaining."

My illustrious pupil worked very hard. She took a sheet of foolscap, copied the text, then wrote it out in Italian, as she heard me pronounce it, with the Italian orthography. Above this she would have another line, with marks up and down like crescents, and all sorts of other notes to aid her in getting the right accent. She never was what I should call quite great when she did Lady Macbeth in English; she was too much absorbed in her wrestle with the words. Our "infernal tongue" puzzled her from first to last. I find allusions to it as a sort of obsession in many of her innumerable letters that promise, at the beginning, to be all about something else. Take this, for instance, sent to me in America after a successful tour. I translate, of course :

New Schools for Old

" We've received the papers, and have all been with you in your happiness. We see your great future, dear. You so deserve a happy fate, that in truth you will not have stolen it when it comes. Just think of your delight in having your mother with you. Oh! if I could only be with you two months. I'm sure I should learn the whole part of Lady Macbeth. Others have offered to teach it to me, but I have not the confidence that they would be like your mother (who had to take my place for the moment). She is so patient, intelligent, correct, artistic, and I will say ' mechanical ' because no other word will express my idea. To teach a tongue as difficult as that of the ancient English poetry, you must know the structure of the throat and palate ; so, ' mechanical ' seems to be the word I want."

This lets us down gently, but here, again, *à propos* of nothing in particular, she raps out :

" Who knows what you may have been thinking of my silence ? But you—naughty one—have not even thought of asking me the reason ! Your triumphs have erased my memory from your thoughts—is it not so ? Ah ! I'm delighted with your magnificent success in Paris, but I am not in the least astonished ; yet allow me to tell you all the same that your English language is diabolically diabolical ! I miss you so much ! I kiss you with all my heart ; and I love you, and am, your Adelaide Ristori."

The grievance, however, was forgotten when the following came, with the present of a lap writing-desk with white and blue violets painted in a lovely cluster on the enamelled lid :

" What a pleasure if you could only come here to see us, and pass days and days with us in this lovely villa !

Both Sides of the Curtain

You should lead a country life. Rising at six and retiring at half-past nine. We have fields, a little orchard, a beautiful little house covered over with roses; and we would enjoy ourselves; and we would laugh!"

We corresponded for years, writing to each other every week. When I last saw her in Rome, in the year of her death, she was still the same loving friend, although her memory was very capricious, and from one moment to another she would forget. She had been a very tall woman, but she seemed to have shrunk into herself, and I was obliged to stoop to kiss her. In my life's gallery of the dear and true she stands among the first.

Her beautiful daughter, Donna Bianca, as she was called, though her proper title was Marchesina, never married; her son George took to art. They were all at court, and he is still one of the court functionaries. Her daughter was engaged to a Roman prince, but he died before the day fixed for their union. She was broken-hearted, said she would never marry, and kept her word. She devoted her life to her mother and never left her. I see her every time I go to Rome—a charming woman—mellowed by suffering rather than by years. Her father was the youngest-looking man, for his age, I ever knew. When he had turned fifty I once saw him and his son out together, and at a little distance wondered which was father and which was son.

One year when I was in Rome with her, the Sicilian players were there. I asked my friends if they were worth seeing; the answer invariably was,

Alla sua cara
Mme Genova... Guerbel
ricordo di stima e affetto
dalla sua

Adelaide Ristori
Del Grillo

New Schools for Old

"*Terza classe.*" Next year this third-class company came to London, and the English public almost lost its wits over them. It is a way they sometimes have with their imports in foreign talent. I went to see them, and after the first act I said to Mr. Vedrenne, who was in a box with me, "Am I in a lunatic asylum?"

"I know where we should be," he replied, "if we attempted to do anything of the kind—in jail."

They were of the ordinary peasant type, and raw in their stage play as the most sordid criminals of real life. They might all have been members of the Mafia; they bit each other, they grovelled on the floor; it was realism studied in the shambles, and saved only from being utterly ridiculous by being utterly disgusting. It was love treated as a disease. The heroine goes to bed over it, claws her own face when there is no other at hand, and literally takes the floor at full length when the paroxysms come on. The neighbours drop in to consult over it, as they might over any other bodily affliction: one is for a mustard plaster, another for a medal of a saint or any other charm. "Put it under the pillow when she's not looking and she'll be all right in the morning." Yes, but get it under the pillow if you can. As they approach the sprawling hoyden, hoping she may have sunk into a doze, she suddenly darts on them with tooth and nail ready for action, and the room was cleared in a trice. The hero, who is in much the same case, jumps on his rival's back, and in this position of mastery bites him in the neck and ear. If you don't exactly come away from it with the passions purified by pity and terror, you at least come away ill. No one would have them for a return journey: the craze was over and the reaction had set in.

True art, of course, knows nothing of these abominable tricks. It suggests and leaves it there, always with the well-known reserve of the sculptor of the Laocoon group. Think of these Sicilians of drama with such a chance in hand. The serpents would not be merely killing their victims, they would be swallowing them whole, and "swellin' wisibly" with the legs and arms half-way down.

Ristori and Salvini were artists to the finger tips, and truly great. And yet when Salvini made a return visit to England he once played at Drury Lane to £9! The greater the artist, sometimes, the greater the risk of being taken up and taken down in this way. On one occasion, when Salvini was playing Othello, I happened to sit next to a young couple duly provided with books of the play in Italian and English. They were deeply immersed in the text, but reading the third act, whilst he was playing in the second! The girl said wearily: "Why did we come?" The young man replied, "Oh, mother says it's so fine." These books of the play what a nuisance they are, a thousand pages turning like one, though not always at the same page. But they are inevitable in certain cases, no doubt.

Ristori, with all her devotion to her art, could enjoy a joke at her own expense, when that, too, was art of its kind. When the great tragi-comic actor Robson burlesqued her as Medea she went to see him, and was most enthusiastic over the performance. She told me it was one of the greatest pieces of acting she had ever seen.

The greatest actor I ever saw in my life was Modena, at the Scala in Milan. He was at that time eighty years of age, and was playing *Louis XI*. I have seen many in this part, including Irving and Charles Kean, but Modena was head and shoulders above them all. It was wonderful. Of course, he appeared only in a special performance, for he had long retired from the stage.

Still thinking in the terms of persons as the best clue to an estimate of the methods of art, I come to some great American players I have seen. Of all these, to my mind Jefferson was the greatest, as being the most human. I often saw Clara Morris play: she was a very remarkable actress and had the gift of tears, without always having to shed them on her own account. It was her fond belief that she merely had to set the example, and that her admirers simply followed, but in this opinion she did less than justice to her own powers. I once saw her in a death scene, leaning on her cushions, surrounded by sorrowing relatives, and with a whole "crying audience" in front. While these were enjoying themselves in their way, she was making comic remarks behind her handkerchief to the actors round her! On another occasion, in her performance of *East Lynne*, she sat at table with the children in the well-known pathetic scene, when she suddenly discovered that she was wearing the wrong shoes. She left the table and went to the door at

Both Sides of the Curtain

the back, called for her shoes, and, holding on by
the curtain, changed them and returned to her
seat—the audience taking it all as part of the business, and weeping it through from first to last. It
was a *tour de force* of audacity, talent and self-
possession all the same. She was essentially American, especially in speech. She often thought of
coming over to England, but her accent was so
marked that it would have spoiled everything for
English ears.

I knew Edwin Booth well: he was another of
our great actors. His Hamlet and his Richelieu
were particularly fine. He was a most charming,
genial gentleman. The great tragedy of his life was
his brother's murder of President Lincoln. The
murderer, Wilkes Booth, was undoubtedly mad.
Edwin retired from the stage for over a year, and
was with difficulty persuaded to resume his career;
but all America stood by him in these trying circumstances, and had the greatest sympathy for him.
I remember a very pleasant time I had in Scotland
with him and his wife. We had a picnic and spent
happy days together.

For some years Lester Wallack's theatre was
the best comedy theatre in New York. He was a
very handsome man, but not a great actor. But he
was surrounded by good players and adored by the
ladies, so all went well.

I am inclined to say that, after Jefferson, William Gillette is the most perfect American actor it
has been my good fortune to see. The latest critique
of his latest creation in America is worth quoting,

as giving one secret of his extraordinary effect upon an audience:

The acting methods made famous through *Sherlock Holmes* and *Secret Service* are concentrated here in most interesting fruition. Effects are created by deft inflections of tone, economy of gesture, and by facial expression. The greatest of these effects is the illusion that the actor is constructing his lines as he goes along. That illusion is rare. There are so many actors who memorise their parts only to read them night after night.

In one word, Gillette never talks like a book in the sense of an unhesitating possession of his text—as all but the best of us are sometimes apt to do. He pauses from time to time, as though for a suitable expression of a sudden thought, as all of us do in real life.

The audiences of those earlier times were sometimes a trial, especially in what was then the back country, when they were prone to revert to the condition of children of nature on the slightest provocation. On my first visit to Chicago with *Forget-me-not* I had a curious reception on my first appearance, and a very odd view of a large portion of the audience. As I entered there was a vision of human backs; every man's face was turned from me, in a rapid scuttle towards the doors. In a few minutes half the seats were empty. The ladies remained, but their heads were turned after their retreating friends, and my welcome seemed chilly indeed, what with the flight of the one sex and the cold shoulders of the other. I remained dumb for a while, but then came a whisper from the wing:

Both Sides of the Curtain

"Don't be frightened, there's been a difficulty in front, but it's over and they're coming back." They did come back, and that with an enthusiastic welcome. I found out afterwards that the "difficulty" consisted of an exchange of revolver shots —happily without serious results; but the prospect of a free fight and a real one had been too much for the western mind.

I have appeared in two of Ibsen's pieces—*Pillars of Society* and *John Gabriel Borkman*—in the last of which I played an exceedingly difficult part, which I hope I succeeded in making an effective one. There was very little in these pieces that was obscene. I was asked to play in *Ghosts,* but that I absolutely refused, for the thing should never have been staged. Ibsen has done harm to the English stage, but the bane and antidote come together, for the audiences at large—I am speaking of the vast majority—will not have him at any price. They may or may not be right, but theirs is the casting vote: it is the twelve men in the box against the pundits of the Bench and Bar. One of our authors, who has written fine comedies on his own account, is now waist deep in the Serbonian bog under this fatal influence. The select few in criticism, who tried to give Ibsen the benefit of a great push in 1897, were simply foiled all along the line. The critics were crushing. They praised us all as actors, and then fell to work on the piece with tooth and claw. We played at the Strand, though "trading" as the New Century Company, which was without a local habitation. *The Times* led the note of depreciation:

New Schools for Old

" The whole atmosphere of the play is that of a tomb, where never a wholesome breath of air circulates, and it is with an inexpressible sense of relief that one sees the curtain fall. *John Gabriel Borkman* is, in short, a nightmare of a play, which would give the horrors to a healthy minded pit and gallery. Ibsen's exposition of his subject in the first act is interesting enough, but the continued oppressiveness, the hopeless pessimism of the story, which is as unlike real life as the wildest romance, ends by shaking the strongest nerves. If this is to mark a new era in theatrical affairs, as the title of the society would imply, then amusement or entertainment in association with the stage is a vain word."

This seemed very happily to characterise its atmosphere as of a Scottish mist in the Shades. *The Daily Telegraph* followed on the same side :

" It was charged to the full with sublimated selfishness, and moans and groans and wrecked lives and defiant egotism! It was a treat to leave a grim and darkened theatre, and to meet healthy, cheery, buoyant life again, where all was bustle and activity, and boys were shouting about cricket and exhibiting placards tempting one to the study of Abel's score.

*   *   *   *   *

" In reading the play there are certain scenes that are stimulating and interesting. These same scenes when acted become trivial or commonplace, depressing or dull. The last of all, the union of the two sad women over the dead body of their selfish hero, is tragedy illumined with poetry. It rings in the ears and haunts one like little Eyolf's crutch. It is a sad antiphonal wail that the reader cannot get out of his ears :

" ' We two sisters—over him we both loved,
    We two shadows—over the dead man.'

Both Sides of the Curtain

"But in the play, as acted, these illumined touches come like flashlights in such a dull morass of tedium that it requires actors of the greatest experience and tact to make them felt, or to divorce them from ridicule. Luckily, those actors and actresses were present yesterday, and they certainly with heroic effort gave occasional life and colour to the very dullest and most deplorably monotonous of all the Ibsen plays yet seen in London.

*　　*　　*　　*　　*

"We are discussing it now as a stage play, as a work framed for and invented for the theatre, as a something that is to revolutionise our old-fashioned, obsolete, ridiculous and conventional forms of dramatic art. As such we have no hesitation in saying that it is perfectly useless, perhaps the worst possible specimen of the master's theory, the greatest 'swashing' blow to the disciple's faith. It fails in that important essential which the drama, viewed in any light, imperatively demands—contrast. A play is not a bad play because it contains one bad man or a dozen, one vile woman or twenty; it may be a very good play in which evil overwhelms good. But it must have contrast. Viewed as works of art, goody-goody or ultra-sentimental plays are as indefensible as plays of pure pessimism and mental as well as moral disease. But they cannot interest if they harp on one string and ring eternally the old tune. Contrast and variety they must have.

*　　*　　*　　*　　*

"Let us take the characters in the play. John Gabriel Borkman, formerly managing director of a bank, caught red-handed in fraud, guilty of unjustifiable acts of peculation, sent to prison after having ruined the widow and orphan, and beggared his own family, comes out of jail to boast about his power, his ambition, his defiance of society, and prates about self and what he intended

198

to do for his fellow creatures and humanity, with misery strewn before his very eyes. Pecksniff is a joke in moral obliquity and turpitude to the Danish banker. Next comes Mrs. Borkman, hard, cold, pitiless, unforgiving, unwomanly and fiendish in most of her actions, but redeemed alone by her insane and animal love for her son, whom she would ruin and incarcerate and drive to desperation, killing the very ' love life ' in him as surely as it was slaughtered in her twin sister, by the fraudulent and impudently defiant banker.

*   *   *   *   *

" Dull and depressing as the play was, it was superbly acted, notably by Miss Geneviève Ward and Mr. W. H. Vernon, who represented the ill-starred husband and wife, convict and enforced widow. They were both of special value in that they determined to *act* Ibsen—to act him thoroughly according to their lights and experience. In later days these Ibsen plays have been taken in a monotonous sing-song fashion, and consistently treated in a kind of Danish Gregorian chant. It seemed imperative to bind them to a formula which required antiphonal chanting rather than acting. Miss Geneviève Ward broke down the tradition in five minutes. She began to act, not to sing, and she acted so remarkably well that she paralysed the Ibsen tradition of acting art, which is to be as morbid, mournful, and unnatural as possible."

The Standard was equally repelled by the awful remoteness of it from life as it is lived, alike by the best and the worst:

" Dr. Ibsen is supposed to be a teacher, but what he is endeavouring to teach here, how any human being can be the better or the wiser for an introduction to John Gabriel Borkman, is a mystery not to be fathomed. The people of the play live and move and have their being in

Both Sides of the Curtain

a world apart, which seems to have no relation to the world in front of the footlights. The effect they create is that of an ugly dream. Everything that was possible appeared to have been done for the representation of the work. Miss Geneviève Ward as Mrs. Borkman and Miss Elizabeth Robins as Ella threw themselves into their parts with a sincerity and earnestness, a thoughtfulness and regard for the task they had undertaken, which was pathetic, considering how small were the results they could by any possibility achieve."

I have dwelt at some length on these notices because I think they put the case against Ibsen very clearly from the English point of view. The English audiences will never take to him. I have talked a good deal with playgoers and critics, and I should think that what precedes and what follows would fairly represent their views.

Their supreme difficulty about the Ibsen plays is that they are not the fish, flesh, or fowl of character and conception. At every turn the personages are ready to double the part of the mooniest of mystics with something exactly opposite. The baffled plain dealer of drama never knows where to have them, because they are not of flesh and blood. " The earth hath bubbles as the water hath, and these are of them." They are but the bondslaves of the plot. At one moment Borkman is a hard-headed, over-bearing Jeremy Diddler of the most sordid description ; at the next he is spouting in this fashion :

" I seem to touch them, the prisoned millions ; I can see the veins of metal stretch out their winding, branching, luring arms to me. I saw them before my eyes like living shapes that night when I stood in the strong-room with the candle in my hand. You begged to be liberated, and I tried to free you. But my strength failed me; and the treasure sank into the deep again. But I will whisper it to you here in the stillness of the night. I love you, as you lie there spellbound in the deeps and the darkness! I love you, unborn treasures, yearning for the light! I love you with all your shining train of power and glory! I love you, love you, love you!"

It is a question as to which will you have: you can't possibly have both. The last, in relation to a creature of this description, seems to be a pure bathos of the first. And, unluckily, this sin against congruity is no incident; it runs through all Ibsen's work. His male characters, especially, are too commonly ready to rise at a bound from the level of vulgar cheats and impostors to the mount of prophecy. It all bespeaks, to the British mind, a very primitive society of little interest to a more complex one. With their wealth, success and standing in life, our audiences despise the penury of circumstance, the dreary procession of the first families of Little Pedlington offered as an equivalent for all outdoors.

In spite of the pretentious setting of mountain and fiord, the human setting is provincial to the last degree. The plot is the intrigue of the sewing class and the Dorcas meeting. Instead of the mighty figures of the old tragedy—kings, heroes, priests—we have the master builder, the petty company promoter in for a deal, the local Chadband. And, for the scope of the action, the suburban township, the tea meeting and the school treat, instead of the wide,

wide world. Drab for its local colour, with never a touch of anything brighter to reflect the light that gives the pulse to life.

The critic of *The Sunday Times* had the *mot* of the situation :

First Servant : My lord, you nod, you do not mind the play.

Christopher Sly : Yes, by Saint Anna, do I. A good matter, surely ; comes there any more of it ?

Page : My lord, 'tis but begun.

Sly : 'Tis a very excellent piece of work, madam lady ; would 'twere done.

Ibsen never rallied on the English stage after that decisive blow.

CHAPTER XIII

MANAGERS AND ACTOR-MANAGERS

THE line of eminent managers, or actor-managers, begins, as I have already shown, with Macready, though Phelps, who succeeded him, brings it as a starting-point within my own experience. I never saw Macready: it is one of the disappointments of my career. I have travelled so much that I had to miss many opportunities of that kind. He it was who really led the way in the revival of Shakespeare on our stage. Charles Kean, with all his merits, was but a follower. My only consolation is that within the last few years I have had the good fortune to meet General Nevil Macready, the tragedian's youngest son, and the General's daughter, both of whom I now count among my dearest friends. General Macready is so very human in private life that one can hardly realise his high position, and that one is talking to the Adjutant-General of the Forces in the present terrible war. But the other day he sent me two fine volumes of his father's diaries, edited by William Toynbee, with the following note:

"DEAR MISS WARD,

"Will you do me the pleasure of accepting these volumes from one whose greatest pride it is to be descended from the profession of which you are so bright an ornament?   " Yours very sincerely,

"N. MACREADY."

Both Sides of the Curtain

Thanks to these, the great actor seems to live before me as I read, and I can almost fancy that I see his rendering of *Virginius*. Such diaries are part of the education of every actor worthy of the name. No wonder it was the writer's lot to be envied as well as admired: so things go too often in real life. The terrible Forrest riots of 1849 in New York form the case in point. Forrest had failed in England, and looking round for a victim, as unhappily " it was his nature to," he found the actor who had charmed both hemispheres ready to his hand, and in both pursued him with the utmost fury of hate. It is useless to go back in any detail to that thrice-told tale of shameful riot, with bloodshed almost on the epic scale. To the honour and glory of America the intervention of the authorities had but one object, to give the British actor a fair hearing and to save his life.

It was more than a struggle between two artists: the real issue was a conflict between two schools. Forrest was a powerful player, but his style seemed to age in a night when Macready came upon the scene. The former tore his passion to tatters, as though he had lost—if he ever had it—all sense of the finer and the more intellectual resources of the art. I saw him when I was quite a girl, and, strangely enough, in the very piece, *Virginius*, in which I could only imagine the man he had determined to regard as his enemy. He had a tremendous voice. We were in a box commanding a view of the wings, and we could see him right at the back, before he came on for a powerful scene. He stood there gesticulating, stamping, and generally working himself up into a positively savage excitement for his rush on the stage. It was as though the Bull of Bashan had been included in the cast, and was doing his best to supply the want of a lashing tail. Even in the then immature stage of my critical faculties, I am bound to say I derived more amusement than instruction from the whole performance.

It was my privilege once to play with Phelps in *The Stranger*, when he was an old man. I appeared as Mrs. Haller, the heroine of that dismal and now discredited piece. I was rather in terror; I had been told that he was exceedingly disagreeable, but I found him quite the contrary. Much to the amazement of the manager and the whole company, he even took me in front of the curtain with him. One must speak of a man as one finds him, but I cannot for the life of me understand why he should ever have been less than kind to Madge Robertson. Yet we have it on her own authority, in her delightful "Dramatic Opinions," that he very nearly missed a ducking for his unmerited coldness towards her when she was working her way up in the profession. Here is her account of the incident :

"At Hull I played Lady Macbeth with Mr. Phelps. The reason I played Lady Macbeth was that there was nobody else to play it, except a very old lady. Mr. Brough told Mr. Phelps that he had better take me, as, whether I could do it or could not, I had at that time so completely got the Hull people to like me that they would forgive me anything. I was put in a garment of my mother's.

Both Sides of the Curtain

I went on, and was received tremendously, and, having been taught by my father, I suppose I got through it somehow, and was vociferously cheered. I was called over and over again. Mr. Phelps did not take me before the curtain. Why should he? When he went on again he was greeted with the most tremendous cries of 'Bring her out!' As my father was standing at the wings he was sent for, and a very young man out of the gallery, of enormous size, came round and said to him: 'Ay, Mr. Robertson, if thou say'st t'word, I'll duck him in t'Humber; he's not brought on our Madge.' My father had to take Mr. Phelps out of the front door to avoid the gallery boys throwing him in 't'Humber.' "

Such treatment of her must always have been inexcusable. I first met her at a luncheon party when I was playing Queen Katharine in Calvert's revival of *Henry VIII.*, and a sympathy seemed to spring up between us at once which has culminated in a lasting friendship. I had previously seen her on the stage, when she was playing Galatea at the Haymarket Theatre, so I can frankly say I had lost my heart to her before we became acquainted, for a more exquisite performance cannot be imagined. She is certainly the greatest English *comédienne*— in the ample French sense of the term—of our time, and she is also a great stage manager. To see her in this capacity is a liberal education in stagecraft. It was on the cards that I might have had the privilege of acting with her at the period I mention. The Bancrofts were going to produce *Diplomacy* at the Prince of Wales's Theatre, and she wrote at once to tell them that she had found the ideal Countess Zika in Miss Geneviève Ward. To my great regret the answer was returned that Mrs. Bancroft was going to play the part herself.

Her story of her wedding is one of the prettiest I know of, on or off the stage. It was a marriage without the honeymoon, as she has told me herself. However, the honeymoon was only postponed by a few weeks; and it may be said to have ended only by the bridegroom's recent death in the fullness of years. Here it is in her own words:

"We were married at Manchester. In those days Henry Compton, the old comedian, was at Manchester for a month—the time the Haymarket company remained there. There were always the plays chosen in which he was the principal person—*The Poor Gentleman*, *The Heir at Law*, *Speed the Plough*, *The Honeymoon*. I thought that, as I should not act for three weeks certainly, and perhaps for a whole month, Mr. Kendal and I would get married; so on August 7 we were married at St. Saviour's Church. The day before that Mr. Mackenzie, Henry Compton's brother and the father of Morell Mackenzie, the throat specialist, was dying, and Compton was telegraphed for to his brother's side. This raised a difficulty for Mr. Buckstone, as the only Shakespearean part with which he could go on at very short notice was Touchstone. On our returning from the church to our lodgings we were told that we had to act Rosalind and Orlando that very night. We had imagined that our marriage was a dead secret, as my husband had got a special licence and we never spoke of it to anybody, except to my parents—my mother in particular, who gave me away. My consternation was overpowering when, in the scene when Rosalind says, 'I take thee, Orlando, for husband,' the house cheered. So our secret was out. At the end of the performance Mr. Buckstone sent for me and asked what I meant by getting married while under contract to him—signed by my father—as a single girl, adding that, by breaking it, I had forfeited my engagement. But, after frightening me very much, he burst into laughter and wished me every happiness, and said that the engagement would go on. In those days engagements were made for three years with a rise of salary of sometimes £2, £5 or £10 a week. On that very day it was my husband's good fortune to have his raised by £5 per week, though, for the moment, he had quite forgotten all about that. So, on the following pay day the £5 came in as a sort of wedding present of which we had never dreamed. In the following week, however, I did not play at all, as Mr. Compton came back and resumed *Speed the Plough*.

"Mr. Buckstone was a kindly man in every sense of the word, and his interest in us never ceased, and it is to this day a delightful remembrance. He was always complimentary, and never forgot to come down to the wings whenever I played Rosalind to hear me sing 'When daisies pied.' In any play, indeed, in which I had a song he used to say, 'Let me know, my dear; I like to hear you.' He was reported to be very deaf, but he invariably heard when he wanted to; and I fancy he used his supposed infirmity as an expedient against bores. He could keep his own counsel as well as anyone. One day, after Gilbert's play, *The Wicked World*, we changed our dresses and had new ones, and I told Mr. Buckstone I did not like mine. He said, ' You don't like your new dress, do you? I never did— and this I like less.' It was Buckstone's youngest daughter who sat to Millais for that lovely picture of ' Cinderella,' and the artist chose her on my recommendation. Buckstone had an enormous family, and on his benefit night at the Haymarket Theatre they used to sit in the Royal box together, dozens of them, of all ages. He always made a speech, and then all the children threw him little bouquets of different sizes, according to their age.

" He was invariably more than kind to me; after my success in Galatea he put my name in large letters on the bill, making me a star, gave me the star dressing-room, and sent me a cheque for £100. He told me that just before the production of *Pygmalion and Galatea*, he feared he would be made bankrupt, and the play had saved him. I was then earning £12 a week, but I suppose the dear old gentleman thought he must do something more. I was so delighted that, when I came on in the second act, I looked at him and said, ' Are *you* a man?' while tears of gratitude rained down my face.

" It is worth recording that the Haymarket Company always rehearsed *The School for Scandal* from Sheridan's original MS.

" Many people probably do not know that Mr. Buckstone personally translated plays from the French and wrote a great many himself. In two of these, *Married Life* and *Single Life*, there were respectively five married and five single couples. I played with him in both—the young girl in *Single Life* and the old governess in *Married Life*. This had originally been played by Mrs. Frank Matthews, a well-known and celebrated character actress. Mr. Buckstone was good enough to say, though I was only about twenty-two at the time, that I had realised his ideal of the part. My good fortune consisted in being a bit of a mimic, for I had based my rendering of the character on the study of a very old-fashioned music mistress of whom I had lessons. You see, I was rather a spoilt child. They used to call me at the Haymarket Theatre 'The Daughter of the Regiment,' because Mr. Chippendale and Mr. Compton had both been actors in my father's theatres.''

The Kendals were the first to restore the fortunes of the St. James's Theatre after it had fallen on evil times, and Sir George Alexander has completed the work. His career as actor-manager has been one of the most brilliant on the contemporary stage. This is due to his personal qualities, and particularly to his unfailing tact, as well as to his mastery of his art. He "has a way with him."

In December, 1915, he called on me one day with a manuscript under his arm and asked me if I would read it, and if I liked the part of the duchess, would I play it? I had not any intention of resuming my stage life at that time, but, being entirely alone in my little home, I felt that if I had some active work it would help me to bear the strain of the war. Moreover, I thought the part of the duchess very pretty, and that it would be really child's play to me after playing tragedy all my life. So I agreed, and thus made my first appearance as a *comédienne* on January 6, 1916, under the most courteous and kind of managers, who seems to have no thought for himself, but always for others. The play was a success at the first, but there came the terrible Zeppelin scare, and this, with bad weather and Lent supervening, was all against us. We ran well over a hundred nights in London, but a trip to Bournemouth ended the career of *The Basker*. The play was beautifully dressed. Sir George Alexander is fortunate in having for helpmate his charming wife, whose energy and intelligence and wonderful taste in art are all of great use to him.

Here, I thought, will be the last appearance of Geneviève Ward on any stage, the more so as I hate formal " Farewells." But Alexander and Louis N. Parker had decreed otherwise, and one day I received a little note from Alexander when he was on tour:

"DEAR FRIEND,

"I am sending you a wonderful play with a wonderful part for you. You will be great in the second act. Please let me know what you think of it."

I told him I thought I could make something of it, and when he came back to town we began to rehearse, and the play was produced January 25, 1917, with enormous success, in which we long luxuriated.

How, I ask, is any daughter of Eve to resist

such temptations (pretty clothes into the bargain) merely to keep a promise to herself?

Add to this the touching ceremony on the stage some nine weeks later—March 27—when the company assembled to offer me congratulations on my birthday in a beautifully illuminated address with these charming lines:

TO GENEVIÈVE WARD

ON HER EIGHTIETH BIRTHDAY

Not eighty winters, four times twenty springs,
Have filled your soul with fair imaginings,
These in your turn you've lavished on mankind
By Beauty, Grace, and Genius refined.
From song to speech you passed, from grave to gay,
Triumphed in opera, queened it in the play;
Roamed the wide world, high priestess of our Art,
There and in King Street conquering every heart.
Each of us murmurs—Happy be your lot—
God ward you—Geneviève—Forget-me-not.

LOUIS N. PARKER.

Percy Macquoid
    des.

followed by the names of the company. The ode again figured, in the autumn of 1917, at a benefit performance at the Theatre Royal, Nottingham, in aid of the Comfort for Troops Fund, and the Lord Roberts Nottingham Hostel—with a motto, "Cheerfulness is the sunny ray of life," from the pen of the heroine of the occasion.

There is another Alexander, too, besides the actor and the manager, and that is the citizen. He

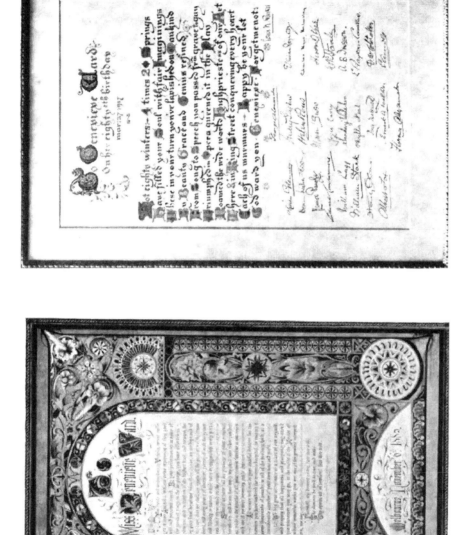

has done good work on the London County Council. He speaks well and gracefully, and his impromptus are achieved without the aid of a prompter. Only the other day, at a meeting of the Actors' Association, he made a capital speech against the attempt to rope into the ranks, as employees, all the humblest workers at the theatre. This would close the houses at once, and the actors' occupation would be gone. Besides, it would be their turn next, and then what would become of a calling that ought to be regarded as one of the services necessary to the well-being of the community? This aptitude for the platform as well as for the boards is only too rare in the profession. We want fair play all round, alike for masters and men; and as the law itself is prone to help only those who are able to help themselves, we shall never get it without champions from our own ranks. Why differentiate against the arts? A few years since a judge laid down the monstrous proposition that a star of opera who had broken an agreement ought not to be held to his bargain, because, by the very nature of his calling, he enjoyed the freedom of the birds who " sang on every tree." Fudge!

In short, as I have said, Sir George has a way with him in everything he says and does. His social gifts are as marked as those peculiar to his calling. See how nicely he contrived to say a cheering word to me when he heard that I had broken fresh ground and was " writing a book." I must quote it for its grace of expression, apart from its highly flattering compliment to myself:

Both Sides of the Curtain

"Your book will not be an entirely satisfactory one, I feel sure, without some eulogy written by one who has been your friend and fellow-worker since the year 1890, and who owes you gratitude in both spheres. As a youthful manager, embarking on a troublesome sea, you taught me courage, and courage has been one of the strongest features throughout your own life. You have had the courage to be sincere in your Art and in your Friendships (my wife and I can bear witness to that). Now, in the Autumn of your career, you are a noble example to the younger generation of Actors and Actresses, and your good influence on them and on the British stage cannot be over-estimated. It is easy enough to be amiable, but it is given only to the few to be great, and greatness belongs to you."

He is certainly sincere in his own friendships, and without any distinction between good hap and ill hap in mere success. I know of a case in which he was prodigal in little flattering attentions to a lady who had fallen on rather hard times in her life as an artist. He had first met her when they were both members of the circle of the late Lady Freake, the Macænas of young people in all the arts who were only hoping to arrive. He lost sight of her for some years, but he took care to have a stall at her disposal whenever she expressed a wish to see one of his plays. She was a bit of a *gourmet*, as well as a patron of the drama on these easy terms. One day, on passing Fortnum and Mason's he was aware of her gazing tenderly at a raised pie in the window, as one who had outlived all other illusions. "Why, is that you?" he said, and she turned to renew the acquaintance with his hearty shake of the hand and a chat about old times. The next day a parcel arrived at her studio, and in it, "With the compliments of George Alexander," was the raised pie. It was prettily done!

We all felt glad of his knighthood as a distinction well earned, and as a compliment to his comrades as well as to himself.

This and Benson's were the two most popular honours in my professional recollection. There was a rather amusing incident in connection with the latter. There was no sword at hand, as the ceremony took place at the theatre in the King's box. But where there's a will there's a way: a man was sent to a theatrical costumier's to procure a property weapon, and Benson was knighted by His Majesty with that. I think this is the only time such a thing has occurred.

It is useless to try to double the parts of actor and of actor-manager unless Nature has had a hand in the work. Most of the best actors have been content to remain actors and nothing else; most of the best managers have recognised the same limitation to their energies, if not always to their powers. Mr. Vedrenne is a striking example of this singleness of aim: he manages; his partner, Mr. Eadie, plays. The former makes no secret of his ambition to establish in England a theatre that may favourably compare with the Comédie Française in its best days; by that I mean not only a theatre where the finest performances can be given, but an organisation embracing all the details of dramatic work —a conservatoire for the training of students, painting-rooms, furniture and property supplies, and, above all, a financial organisation that will ensure pensions to artists on their retirement. It is a great purpose, and he has already gone no inconsiderable way towards its realisation. He thinks that London, the greatest and wealthiest city in the world, should have such a theatre; and, in the old days at the Court, Granville Barker and he went into the matter very seriously. Since then a committee has been formed for "The National Theatre," but what the results of their efforts may be has yet to be made known. He has tried as much as he could to produce British works, and to help in every way British authors, actors and actresses; and this applies equally to the Vedrenne-Barker management as to the Vedrenne and Eadie of the present day.

In 1916 Mr. Vedrenne offered, as a prize at the School of Dramatic Art, to find an opening for a young lady in his company for a year, if allowed to make his selection. This was done, and the winning candidate has been with him, playing small parts, ever since, and is doing quite well. In April of 1917 the competition took place again, with every promise of the same result. He hoped that other managers might take the same course, but as yet they have not followed suit.

He takes a special pride and delight in casting pieces and in discovering new authors, actors and actresses. His own public confession of faith shows that few theatres in London are more interesting to the playgoer who believes in English drama than the little Royalty in Dean Street, where, in 1911, he

Photo: L. Caswall Smith.

AS MARGARET OF ANJOU IN "RICHARD III."

and Mr. Dennis Eadie began their venture together. The former, in addition to much other varied experience, had been jointly responsible, with Mr. Granville Barker, for the most famous chapter in the records of the Court Theatre, an experiment that made theatrical history and gave Mr. Bernard Shaw his public.

At the Court he was concerned in the production of many plays by Shaw, two each by Ibsen and Maurice Hewlett, three of Euripedes, and of other plays by Hauptmann, Schnitzler, Granville Barker, John Galsworthy, Elizabeth Robins, W. B. Yeats, John Masefield and Maeterlinck. The excellence of the acting at the Court became "proverbial," and a column could be filled with the names of the players who "scored." But one may serve : it is interesting to remember that Mr. Dennis Eadie "arrived" under that famous management in such plays as *The Trojan Women, The Return of the Prodigal, The Charity that Began at Home, The Voysey Inheritance, The Silver Box,* and *Man and Superman.* He had, however, made a reputation when the Vedrenne-Eadie management began. In addition to his work at the Court Theatre, he had played at the Kingsway. He was in the original cast of *Waste,* and *Strife;* and at the Duke of York's he had given an exceptionally striking performance as the luckless Falder in Mr. Galsworthy's *Justice.*

Here there is ample "experiment." Mr. Arnold Bennett was new to the theatre, Mr. Macdonald Hastings and Mr. Harold Brighouse were discoveries. *Milestones* was an entirely new form of the dramatic entertainment. So was *My Lady's Dress*. The true has not been forgotten, but the new has been diligently sought.

So with the players. Miss Gladys Cooper was appearing at the Hippodrome when she was engaged by Vedrenne and Eadie, to become, in a few months, a recognised leading actress. The casts have included some of the cleverest and best among the actors and actresses of the day.

English acting never stood on a higher level than it does now, and English players, as has recently been pointed out by Mr. J. T. Grein, need not fear comparison with the players either of France or Germany.

The *Milestones* dinner, in celebration of the first hundredth night of the play, was very interesting. Our hosts were members of the O.P. Club. Lord Howard de Walden was in the chair, and many celebrated people were among the guests. It fell to my lot to make a speech. The youngest actors and actresses of the day were there, side by side with the veterans—some of them, like myself, still "going concerns" as performers who had not yet written *Finis* below the record of their work.

Forbes-Robertson has been more fortunate as an actor than as an actor-manager, but his success on the stage has made ample amends. He was the original Sir Horace Welby in *Forget-me-not*. He had been playing for some few years, but had only achieved small parts with the Bancrofts at the Prince of Wales's, and he told me sadly that he had never had a chance. I had engaged him for my

Managers and Actor-Managers

Lyceum season, and after the failure of *Zillah* I put on *Lucrezia Borgia*. He was one of two young men in my company of whom I knew very little, and I had given the part of Gennaro to the other. Forbes-Robertson wrote me a melancholy letter saying that he always got the worst of it. I replied, fortunately for both of us, that, while I really did not see he had the worst of it, as they were all poisoned in the end, I certainly would do my best to give him a chance, if he could manage to live on to my next venture; and I kept my word. His Sir Horace was a charming performance and brought him to the fore. He was young for the part, which needs a man about forty, but, except for that, he was quite suitable to it. A rather funny thing— in the last act I had to clutch his clothes, as it was a very violent scene, and he complained that I actually tore them. Perhaps I did, for I meant business. Years after, when we were playing together in *King Arthur* at the Lyceum, I sent him anonymously a doll's dress-coat with a note saying that he had outgrown it. I suppose he had forgotten the incident in *Forget-me-not*, and for weeks he was quite perplexed to know who was the donor and what the present meant. I finally enlightened him. I wanted him to continue with me on tour with *Forget-me-not*, but, as he had made his mark as Sir Horace, he thought it would be best for him to remain in London on the chance of getting something in town. I agreed with him, for successes are so quickly forgotten.

As Garrick in the famous picture stands between

Both Sides of the Curtain

Tragedy and Comedy, so Robertson for awhile was in much the same predicament as between pictorial art and the stage. He followed art seriously in his youth, and was a fellow-student of Samuel Butler, the author of "Erewhon." Butler was in the same state of uncertainty about his own career, with less excuse, for literature, and nothing but literature, had manifestly claimed him for its own. *The Way of All Flesh* settled that matter when one day he shyly put a copy of it in Robertson's hand and the latter took it home to his people. They were of critical standing, and they began to prophesy forthwith.

No doubt the system of actor and manager rolled into one may be carried too far. In doubling the parts this composite being necessarily tends to fight for his own hand, and to choose the pieces that suit *him*. It precludes a company of " all the talents," such as the Comédie Française tries to get and very often does. There, the only concern is the piece as a whole and the perfect harmony of its setting. The pieces are not written for the individual actor, nor is his part the dominant factor. He takes, within certain limits, of course, the part assigned to him, and at certain times has a genuine pride in his own humility. Great actors at the Français have occasionally consented to be cast for not much more than, " My lord, the carriage waits." This, when it is all done in good faith and the spirit of brotherhood, sometimes has marvellous results. The piece moves as if on springs that make actors and audiences insensible of a jolt. No one puts in solely for his "bit of fat." The object is to make the team win, not the individual performer. But in these competitive times it requires rare self-denial and great *esprit de corps.* Sarah Bernhardt was unequal to this, and had to set up for herself. So did Coquelin, though not in the same absolutely self-seeking way. He did not leave the company of the Français, but he claimed long periodical "holidays" to enable him to appear elsewhere and make all the money and fame he could get. He became in these intervals a one-man show. Sarah paid for her greed by the decay of her art, until at last all she could say of her glory was "a poor thing, but mine own."

The English actor has the racial passion for independence. He longs to set up for himself. Each separate theatre may, at no distant date, be labelled by a proper name, Brown's Theatre, Jones's Theatre, with Robinson's glaring defiance over the way. The result is not always a happy one, what need to say more? Some of Marie Wilton's best work was done at the little Strand Theatre, when it was a constellation rather than a bright particular star. Benson, whatever he does, never has himself in view at all—except when he shaves. Irving was so much the individual that under "management" he might have died of a broken heart.

CHAPTER XIV

OTHER MANAGERS

THE manager is the product of his time, and no house and no player (with, perhaps, the single exception of Benson) now struggles for the absolute rigour of the game of legitimate drama. Old Drury and Covent Garden were once supposed to be pledged to that crusade, but it was an illusion even in the palmy days. The greatest managers had to make many concessions to the demand for novelty. Macready, the last and greatest of them all, fought the good fight with success, yet his memoirs abound in groans over the necessity of compromise with the frivolities of popular taste. His farewell performance in *Macbeth*, at Drury Lane, had something of the grandeur of a religious ceremony, and his successor, the nimble Bunn, lost no time in trying his luck with a circus under the roof of the old classic fane. Anderson could think of nothing better. E. T. Smith, personally the lowest decline in standing and in dignity, tried music at popular prices, tempered, however, by *Comus* and *King John*. Chatterton was not without great ideas, but he had to pursue them by devious paths that finally led to bankruptcy.

As a "character" in theatrical annals, Smith

was an extraordinary person, a born gambler from the cradle, who scorned the narrow limits of the cards and dice. In all that came under his notice he seemed to seek only the chance of a lucky deal. As he paced the streets—and he had paced them in the way of his duty as a policeman at the outset of his career—he could hardly pass a shop to let without a vision of some new use of it that would make his fortune. He saw in one, which had failed as a pastrycook's, an ideal site for the sale of bonnets, took it, put in a smart business woman as deputy, and netted a handsome profit in no time. Nothing came amiss to him. He founded drinking bars, where ironmongery or dentistry had failed to please. He haunted the auction rooms in his decline, sometimes with a bank-note in his pocket which he had merely hired for the day.

He seems to have taken Drury Lane, as his country took the empire, in a fit of breezy absence of mind. For him the old national theatre was exactly on the same footing of adventure in bargains as the bonnet shop and the bar. As Edward Tyrrel Smith, he claimed descent from an admiral of that name, probably of the old Phœnician service, for his features were decidedly of Semitic cast. I used to hear a good deal about him from the gossip of green rooms, though we never met.

His first theatrical venture of any note was at the Marylebone Theatre, in Church Street, Edgware Road, but it is said that he had previously figured as the manager of a penny gaff. Fortune knocked at his door in a rather singular way. As a constable

on his beat, he had one night to quell a disturbance
in a public-house in Church Street, Edgware Road,
and got severely maltreated. He was carried into
the tavern and put to bed, and he made such good
use of his time with the landlady, a widow of the
" fair, fat and forty " order, that he became in due
course her husband and the landlord. From this to
the Marylebone Theatre was but a step in both
senses of the word.

After some years spent in this venture he felt
strong enough for the flight to Drury Lane. When
that fell away from him he went into other speculations—some theatrical, others of a totally different
kind. The last of any importance was the building
of the Elephant and Castle Theatre, in the New Kent
Road, an undertaking which, he used to say, " broke
his back "—in other words, ruined him as an operator
on a great scale. The net result, however, was retirement on a small competence to the neighbourhood of Kennington Park with another and a more
youthful wife. I do not know her number, nor
perhaps did he.

His stories bearing on his theatrical career were
innumerable, and he was never tired of telling them.
One turned on his having found the happiest of his
ideas for the stage while watching a joint roasting
for his dinner. I give it, as it comes to me, only at
second-hand, and without any attempt to render the
beauty of his diction.

" I was sitting at the kitchen fire one Sunday
morning with Bob Roxby and Bill Beverley, my
scene painter, who had dropped in to help me with

Photo: Ellis & Walery.

AS MARGARET OF ANJOU IN "RICHARD III."

the joint and with an idea for a grand transformation scene for our first pantomime at Drury Lane. We'd said all we had to say for the moment, but we were thinking hard and staring hard at the fire without exactly knowing what we expected to find there. All of a sudden I noticed that the loin of pork—that's what it was—as it caught the fire—drip, drip, looked just like so much golden rain or, better still, in all the colours of the rainbow.

" ' I've got it, boys,' I said, ' if we could only get that effect ! '

" ' Pork and all ? '—but that was only Bob.

" ' Don't be foolish ! '

" But Beverley was another man of genius, and he saw the grandeur of the conception.

" ' I can do it,' he said, and do it he did. The rainbow rain was introduced and caught—faster than the pork—all over the country. But we had it first."

His grand story—for gala days, as one might say—was on the subject of royal patronage.

" I was going along one day, turning over in my mind how I could contrive to get the patronage of Her Majesty Queen Victoria for my benefit at Drury Lane Theatre, when I saw a grand carriage, drawn by a fine pair of horses, coming along at a deuce of a rate. Who should be inside but my old acquaintance Mo' Solomons, the well-known sheriff's officer. I challenged him, of course, and he stopped.

" ' I've just seized this 'ere carriage and 'osses

for debt at the Dook of ——'s,' says Mo, 'and
I'm going to take 'em to some stables I know of
to be took care of till they're sold by auction—
which won't be long first, unless the Dook is pretty
sharp in payin' up.'

"'I wish you'd lend them to me for a bit before
you do that.'

"'Lend them to you! What for?'

"'Look here!' With that I told him how
anxious I was to get Her Majesty's patronage for
my benefit, and how it would serve me if he would
lend me the turn-out for awhile, just as if it was
my own, to enable me to drive up in style to
Buckingham Palace and see Colonel Phipps
about it.

"'Mo' fairly gasped. 'What an idea!' said he.
'Get inside and we'll talk it over; but I don't think
I can let you have the things—it would hardly be
reg'lar.'

"'Reg'lar be hanged!' says I. 'I must go in
state.'

"With that I jumped in, and on the road to
the stables I worked on his feelings as a man. With
this and other inducements he consented to pull up
at Drury Lane. There I picked out two of the
tallest supers I could find—for we were rehearsing
a big piece that day with a lot of supers in it—and
rigged them out in the finest stage liveries in the
wardrobe, with a suit for Mo's man on the box.
Hats and wigs and all the rest of it, including gloves
and silk stockings—Lord! how they all laughed—
supers, coachman and all, for I took them into my

confidence. The coachman was a fat old fellow and he looked grand. With that away we drove to the Palace.

"When we got there, the men on duty, seeing the fine ducal escutcheon on the panels, threw open the door without a word, and out I popped and went in.

"'Who does Your Grace want to see?'

"'Colonel Phipps,' I said shortly, in my best upper-crust manner. 'Urgent importance. He will know.'

"In another moment I was ushered into a fine room where the Colonel was toasting his back at a huge fire and his hands behind him. You should have seen him stare.

"'Who are you, sir, may I ask?' he said at length, with a frigid, Arctic-regions sort of air. 'I thought it was the Duke of ——'

"'I'm the manager of Drury Lane Theatre,' said I promptly, not at all taken aback.

"'The manager of Drury Lane Theatre,' said the Colonel, who was a very prim and starchy old gent. 'And what, pray, does the manager of Drury Lane Theatre want here? What, may I ask, sir, has brought you here in this peculiar manner?' Here he looked very severe and gulped a bit, and pulled at his necktie.

"'I want,' said I calmly, 'to ask if Her Majesty would favour me by extending her patronage to me at my theatre on the occasion of my forthcoming benefit, which comes off——' naming the date.

Both Sides of the Curtain

"The Colonel was aghast, but at last he recovered his breath.

"'Allow me to inform you, sir, that in all matters of this kind it is invariably the custom to approach Her Majesty by way of memorial.'

"'Oh, is it?' said I.

"'It is,' said he; 'it is. Good day.' With that he touched a bell on the mantelpiece and the servant entered.

"'Show this gentleman out,' said the Colonel stiffly, 'and be careful whom you admit to me again.' And he turned on his heel and walked to another part of the room.

"Out I walked too, as cool as a cucumber, and downstairs and out at the door and into the carriage, and away I drove to the theatre, where I had arranged with Mo' to wait for me. There the men got out of their liveries, the coachman resumed his old coat and hat, etc., and away went the carriage and horses to the stables where Mo' meant to put them up.

"After that Mo' and I refreshed and I told him what had passed.

"'But it was false pretences; I wonder he didn't have you locked up,' he said, when we had had our laugh.

"'Sugar,' says I.

"Well, that passed. A long time after, when we had quite a new bill, I received a letter from the Palace, signed by Colonel Phipps, and commanding, in official form, the appearance of Mr. Charles Mathews and the other members of my Drury

Lane Company at Windsor Castle on a certain day.

"Now was my chance. I didn't hesitate a moment, but sat down and wrote this straight off, on a sheet of Drury Lane note-paper:

"'*To Colonel Phipps.*

"'SIR,—In reply to your communication from Her Majesty the Queen, commanding the appearance of Mr. Charles Mathews and the Drury Lane Company at Windsor Castle on the ——, allow me to inform you that it is *invariably the custom to approach the Manager of Drury Lane Theatre by way of memorial.*'

"I never had any reply, and I don't know what the Colonel thought of it, or whether he communicated my answer to Her Majesty or not. And I don't care. But I *do* know that Mr. Charles Mathews and the Drury Lane Company never went to Windsor Castle, and that the Queen never came to Drury Lane Theatre while I was lessee and manager of it. What matter? I had my revenge. I gave Phipps a Roland for his Oliver. He was my mark; I'd no ill-feeling towards the Queen."

It was under Smith's management, old play-goers will remember, that the fine-figured American actress, or only circus rider, Adah Isaacs Menken, appeared at Astley's Theatre in the title part of *Mazeppa, or The Wild Horse of the Ukraine.* It was one of the great equestrian stock pieces long before her time, and an actor named Holloway used to attract large feminine audiences to see him whenever he played the hero—just as Adah Isaacs Menken proved a never-failing draw for audiences of the other sex. She was tall and finely proportioned, though not particularly handsome, but she created quite a sensation nightly as she careered on the back of the steed to which she was lashed, up and down the long and tortuous " rakes " that were set on the huge stage, for the mimic progress of the pair. She had jet black hair, cut short, curled all over, and brought down very low towards the point between the eyebrows, and dark, languorous Jewish eyes—indeed, she was a Jewess—with fine stage features. The rich and glossy flesh-coloured silk tights that encased her splendidly moulded lower limbs, and the snowy white, close-fitting drapery that she wore round her body (all unsoiled by the ghastly ride) contrasted well with the dark colour of the horse and produced a fine effect. But the crowning glory came when, after she was released from the courser, she stood upright and cried:

" Once more I stand erect; once more do I assume the godlike attitude of Freedom and of Man."

The applause, of course, was tremendous, and she was called until they were tired out on both sides.

On the first night the gallant manager was waiting to share her triumph by leading her on. But she soon put him in his place by telling him, in a pronounced American accent, " not to come fussing around." It was his penance for trying to mate with a star.

The lady's tastes were not for theatrical men at all, however important, but for prize-fighters and for writers of note. She was herself the reputed author of a poem, "Infelicia," which *The Tatler* of that day, however, attributed to Mr. Swinburne, who had the honour of her acquaintance. She was at that time the wife of the famous prize-fighter John C. Heenan, the huge opponent of Tom Sayers, and at her hotel near Charing Cross she consorted with a noted champion of England and his cousin (both of gipsy blood), who was her favourite. She died in Paris in the prime of life and was buried there.

Another lady of fine physique who used to play the part of Mazeppa in the provinces with great success quitted the profession, having some property of her own, and for years kept a large boarding-house in Bloomsbury. Little did her guests think, as she sat at the head of her dinner table with the urbanity—not to say the mealy-mouthedness—suited to this trying part, that she had been a very Tartar on the stage.

Smith's successor in the lesseeship of Drury Lane was the manager of his box office, F. B. Chatterton. The promotion turned his head, and his outbursts of wrath behind the curtain were terrible. The humbler members of the company quailed before him. He, however, made a bold attempt to revive the glories of the house, and, as I have said elsewhere, had Phelps, Barry Sullivan, Charles Dillon and Mrs. Kendal on his engagement lists. I played Rebecca in *Ivanhoe* for him there in 1875, but, alas! only as " grand spectacular drama."

Both Sides of the Curtain

His great failure arose through trying to do too much. He undertook to manage three theatres at once and broke down under it. Drury Lane is always said to be enough for any one man, but Chatterton tried his hand at the Adelphi—where I saved *The Prayer in the Storm* when it seemed past praying for—and at the Princess's as well. Since his day London managers have learnt much, and some take theatres by the half-dozen with a light heart. What their American colleagues can do in this line is a calculation almost too great for the ordinary mind.

His last venture of note, after his downfall at Drury Lane, was Sadler's Wells. He tried to make a living there, but in vain—his lucky star had set for ever. At one time a manager might step with more dignity from "the Wells" to "the Lane" than from "the Lane" to "the Wells." Phelps could do either without loss of caste; but then Phelps was Phelps.

Chatterton had a passion for litigation, and he lived to see his folly. When he was mounting *The Forty Thieves* at the Wells, his last venture, he was asked how they were to dress the ballet girls who took the title part. "Dress 'em as lawyers," he growled.

And dressed as lawyers they were, so far as flowing robes and white horsehair wigs were concerned. But the robes were red, as were the bodices, trunks, tights, and shoes—perhaps to convey an idea of the future state of that profession.

The pantomime ran very badly for about six

232

weeks, and then the brokers were put ·in for rent. The porter who held the keys of the house was reluctant to give them up, and sought his master in his private room.

"Am I to part with them, sir?"

There was a moment or two's pause. Chatterton did not speak, and sat with his head leaning on his hands—a sorry sight. Then the once autocrat of Drury Lane said with a sigh: "Yes, old man."

So ended Chatterton's long and busy career as a great London manager. For a short time he fluttered about in the provinces with a travelling company, but did no good.

After his fall his overbearing manner entirely vanished, and he reverted to the obsequiousness of the box office. To many who could hardly get a word from him in his prosperous days he appeared almost unduly humble. Such are the uses of adversity.

Tyrant as he had been, still he had a good heart. He often kept old actors on his staff out of pure kindness. "Why do you do it?" he was once asked.

"Well, if I don't employ them, who will? What are they to do?"

One or two of these—not all—afterwards got into the habit of "seeing him coming" and taking a side street to avoid a meeting.

"Blow, blow, thou winter wind!"

After the mismanagers, as one might call them, came a man who restored the fortunes of Drury

Both Sides of the Curtain

Lane—in his own way, of course. Sir Augustus Harris was a good example of a man who both lost and found himself on the stage. His immediate predecessors never found themselves at all.

I knew him well. He first thought of being an actor, and he made his *début* in that capacity at Manchester in 1878, when I made my own in tragedy with Lady Macbeth. He was the Malcolm of the cast, and very bad at that—so bad that he was the butt of the company for his way of carrying his sword. I tried to console him by telling him that I thought some other kind of venture in drama might be more in his line. So it proved, in the sense in which he took the suggestion. He became the greatest lessee and manager of his day, had plays written for him piping hot with actuality, got others to play in them, and bestrode a narrow world of his creation like another Colossus of the scene. His example showed Frohmann the way to even greater conquests in the same line. Neither could ever have been an actor, both were pre-eminently men of action in stage production, which, it is needless to say, is quite another thing.

There is always something of the dictator in the successful manager. He must know his own mind. The stage behind the scenes is a world of warring ambitions, and there would be no peace were there no Cæsar in the background to keep them under control. *Punch's* title of " Augustus Druriolanus " for Harris was an exceedingly happy thought. In his nature, his powers, and the vast reach of his schemes he was truly of the Imperial line.

234

Other Managers

He began work long before he began breakfast, not only taking time by the forelock, but pulling it hard. The first person to arrive in the morning at " The Elms " was his secretary, Mr. Arthur Yates—a son of the late Mr. Edmund Yates, of *The World*—a polished and urbane person, more closely connected of late years with music-halls than theatres. He brought with him all the latest letters and telegrams from Drury Lane Theatre, and took instructions on them while the chief was gently soaking in his bath. Then came the morning meal, not less important than the correspondence, for Sir Augustus was a mighty trencherman. Then he glanced at the newspapers, and rarely failed to find some flattering article about himself, for his great theatrical and operatic projects kept him constantly in the public mind.

He now turned his thoughts to the work of the day. Perhaps he had some dramatic author staying at the house who was collaborating with him in one of those mechanical and elaborate—yet in many respects happy-go-lucky—productions called " Drury Lane Dramas." If so, there would naturally be important conversations with him. After his patron had left for town, the collaborator, still remaining at the house, would go to his desk and do his best to combine instructions with original ideas. The work turned out on this curious system was naturally wanting in almost every quality of dramatic art, but it usually pleased the public, and that was enough for the authors. The writer's toil was cheered by the certainty that his play would be produced.

Both Sides of the Curtain

One of his authors, E. L. Blanchard, was always sure of a favourable hearing. He was the writer of the annual pantomime for Drury Lane, and had held that office for many years. The whole scheme of it might be pulled about a good deal in rehearsal, but Blanchard retained half the honours at least of the authorship. His life was as delightful as his work, as I can testify, for one of my very interesting friendships was with him and his wife. They were both enthusiastic in good causes. Her special interest was in the work of emigration for women, and she had to her credit the happiness of many a home. Blanchard was a charming writer and a most genial critic, and their home in Adelphi Terrace was the rendezvous of their literary and artistic friends. It was always so very restful for me, when returning from my arduous work on tour, to find these two dear people ready to encourage and to cheer. They were an ideal couple, and there was a romance in their life. They had been lovers in their youth, separated by adverse circumstances, but meeting again in mature age, they found that their love was not dead but only resting, and that if its early glamour of passion had gone, a still sweeter sentiment survived for the marriage that united them at last. I never saw anything more beautiful than their mutual tenderness.

It was now time, perhaps, for the great man's audiences with the managers of his provincial touring business, who came to discuss some grand project for the control of all the great provincial theatres. He had a scheme of this kind well in hand which, if

it had been thoroughly carried out, though it never
was, might have enabled him to demand whatever
terms he pleased of touring companies begging for
"a date." He, however, obtained possession of two
great houses—the Grand, Glasgow, and the Tyne
at Newcastle, and they were carried on for a period,
but, being mere links of a chain that was never completed, they were eventually given up.

For the Grand Theatre he engaged as managing
director for a period of two years, with two more
years to follow should the theatre prove a paying
concern, the well-known Mr. Clarence Holt, an actor
and manager of great experience. All went well for
a time, but one day the autocrat suddenly arrived
in Glasgow, and finding Mr. Holt's portraits all over
the town and his own nowhere, he abruptly dismissed the servant who had become the rival. The
fallen minister threatened an action for unjustifiable
dismissal, but never brought it, for his master was
a sort of theatrical William the Conqueror, against
whom few cared to make a stand. One of his under-
lings, however, an actor, did venture to call him to
order for a discourteous word, and even went so far
as to say that he should expect an apology. What
is more, he nearly got it, so greatly was Harris stag-
gered by the very absurdity of the demand. It
never came, of course, but the sufferer had the spirit
to leave the company.

Another actor, playing in one of the Drury Lane
productions at a suburban theatre at a salary of between thirty and forty pounds a week, found fault
with the dressing-room accommodation, and refused

to go on at night unless he had a room to himself. Sir Augustus explained that it was impossible to grant the request owing to sheer want of space in a house of that class. The actor was obdurate. The incensed chief immediately replaced him by another member of one of the companies, who no doubt had understudied the part, and a very profitable occupation was gone for the rest of the tour.

When presiding at rehearsal he used frequently to lose his temper and rap out at all and several on the stage, from the highest to the lowest, sometimes telling them to consider themselves discharged there and then :

"You think I can't do without you; be off, the lot of you."

And away "the lot" would go, at least, as far as the wings, but only to return a little later on and resume as if nothing had happened. Such dismissals and such returns became at last almost a part of the business of the scene. At pantomime rehearsals he would sit in the stalls with a man beside him bearing a huge pasteboard trumpet, through which, when his chief had become hoarse with bawling, he transmitted the latter's remarks. These sometimes included "language" faithfully repeated, epithets and all.

The ladies of the ballet and "extra girls," as they are generally called, would sometimes give him a Roland for his Oliver in their own way. So I heard from a friend in their confidence who had the story first-hand from one of their number.

"We were at a pantomime dress rehearsal one

day, and Sir Augustus was there. There was a rare lot of us, what with extras, ballet girls and the ' Long Sixes.' ''

" ' Long Sixes,' what on earth are they—tallow candles? ''

" Foolie! The ' Long Sixes ' are extra tall show girls—sort of little giantesses, but beautifully proportioned and very handsome—when they ain't very ugly. Well, we were Amazons, and very lovely we looked in our armour and our helmets and all the rest of it, as much as there was. We had pikes —and pretty sharp they were, though they were only tipped ,with cardboard. Well, the ' Long Sixes ' were leading us on and we had to charge; but we didn't charge in the right direction, and we didn't hold our pikes in the right way—at any rate, to please the Boss. So he told us to hold them lower and make for him for all we were worth. We did, and pinned him right up against a scene where he couldn't get away, and there held him till he begged for quarter.''

" Did he threaten to discharge you? ''

" Oh, no, it was too late to do that—he couldn't have replaced us if he had. He laughed it off and left us the honours of the fray.''

Perhaps he had lunched too well, for he took this meal on a scale that would have made a food crank or a teetotaller faint away. But this gave him great vigour for the time being, and he arrived at the theatre with an energy that was simply appalling. His presence there was immediately felt in every department. Everybody was on the alert, from the old ex-police inspector, who acted as stage door-keeper, down to the charwomen. The stage carpenters, the scene shifters, the property men, the limelight men, the wardrobe women were more in-dustrious—even the scene painters daubed away with greater briskness. The very clock seemed to move faster, and the typewriters in the correspondence de-partment, which led to his private room, to click at the double as he passed.

At the theatre he would remain all day, directing operations, receiving people with whom he had appointments, and with a strong guard between him and the bores. Then perhaps he would have to dash off to a committee meeting at a theatre, other than Drury Lane, in which he had an interest. This done, he returned to resume work in his private room, dic-tating, scheming, overlooking accounts, yet leaving it all suddenly from time to time to dart on to the stage and give an eye to a rehearsal. Back again in his room, perhaps he found another privileged visitor, and in the midst of their conversation he might pause to send an order to the City for shares in a financial undertaking. No wonder that at times he would press his head and say in an agonised way, "I shall go mad! I know I shall go mad."

With his intense restlessness he occasionally drove some of those in his employment half crazy, and he made one gentleman, who was his right-hand man, so unwell with the strain of being always in his company that he had to make periodical visits to Brighton to recuperate. There he was attended by the chief's own doctor, at the chief's expense; but the recovery was rather slow, as all the correspondence relating to his department was still regularly forwarded to Brighton every morning.

He could not always say "no," for all that. When particularly pertinacious ladies came to solicit engagements—and there are many such, that fear no mortal manager, just as there are ladies that fear no mortal editor—he would depute the duty of facing them to a representative, with private instructions to get rid of them as soon as possible. This one, of course, had to bear the brunt of their wrath as the villain of the piece, for standing between them and the fruition of their hopes.

In conducting rehearsals, especially towards the last, he showed immense energy for a short time, and then tired and left someone else to take his place. As the day wore on he had another hearty meal, and then, the office work over, snatched a doze in his room, or sometimes slept for hours. On awaking, he dressed for the evening, and remained at the theatre until the performance came to a close. After that he supped at the Albion, or at a restaurant in Regent Street in which he had a pecuniary interest, and finally went home.

At home it is no exaggeration to say he was always absorbed in work. He would sit up for what was left of the night, planning out some great pantomime, conjuring up all sorts of scenes and situations, and thinking how he could surpass himself and beat his last year's record.

When the pantomime was written he went over it most laboriously with a view to its improvement,

and passed it on to one of the principal managers
for further revision. This done, he took another
turn at it, until what with his cuts, additions and
interlineations, in all sorts of coloured inks, the
manuscript was a mystery to all but the learned in
the craft. Dramas were also treated in the same
way, but not to such an extent. The anguish of
the susceptible author was something excruciating.
A story is told of one Drury Lane playwright, whose
piece had been very freely cut, who used to approach
the stage-manager in confidence with an " Any more
of my stuff gone to-day? "

When he had control of the Glasgow and Newcastle-on-Tyne theatres, he would suddenly take it
into his head to pay a flying visit to one or other
of them. It was down one day and up the next.
One night he turned up unexpectedly at the Grand,
Glasgow, to have a look at a new piece by the late
John Coleman and another author. It was a great
failure, and the house was nearly empty. He sat
for a little time, stared at the performers, looked
round the house in disgust, uttered a few angry
exclamations, and departed. The piece was soon
withdrawn, and Coleman had good cause to know
the reason why.

He was so preoccupied with work that he often
forgot important social engagements through sheer
weariness of brain. One evening he had to appear
at a grand dinner given in his honour. All were
assembled except the guest of the occasion. At
length two of his aides-de-camp set out to look for
him. They found him at home, fast asleep by the

fire—he had forgotten all about the dinner. They roused him, hurried him into uniform, and bore him off to make what excuse he could.

Marvellous was the number of men that he "made" in his peculiar way—hardly heard of before they leapt into notoriety under his banner, and achieving a repute that must have been as great a surprise to themselves as it was to the world. Most of them passed into oblivion after his death. Some tried to "keep up the connection" by imitating his peculiarities of dress, especially in the matter of capes of superfine cloth, lined and faced with satin. In this way there was a distinct Drury Lane livery, and you could tell an important member of the staff at a glance by the cut of his coat.

These were his sycophants who, in his lifetime, lost no opportunity of putting themselves in his way. When he was knighted, a group of them watched for him as he came out of the Albion alone in his glory and in a meditative mood. With one accord they took off their hats and, bowing almost to the ground, said deferentially, "Good morning, Sir Augustus!" The greeting was not returned.

Like his father, a famous operatic stage-manager, he was deeply interested in opera, and he worked incessantly to re-establish it in public favour. He really loved music. He would frequently travel to the Continent, and to parts more "remote," to secure talent. On these occasions he put himself in charge of some trustworthy person to look after him, and to see that he sent to London the cheques required for the several concerns. It was, in a way, like the departure of the great Napoleon for a campaign. His "marshals" stood in groups about the stage door to give him the needful send-off, while Lady Harris, as the Josephine of the occasion, awaited him in her carriage for the drive to the station. Wrapped in his great fur travelling coat, he usually sat subconscious of the interest and attention he excited, yet too much absorbed in his own thoughts to enjoy it to the full.

He began life in the City and formed some methodical habits of business that stood him in good stead to the last. At Drury Lane all the accounts were looked over by a staff of accountants in his employ, and they were very strict in their view of their duties. His sagacious manager-in-chief knew this, and on being pressed by him to take the position of treasurer of the theatre, so as not to sever his connection with the house—for certain changes had taken place which rendered his services in his first office no longer necessary—he shook his head and politely declined. "No, no, thank you!" he said. "I'll be no treasurer to be dragged before your Court of Star Chamber (a caustic allusion to the body of accountants) whenever they think proper, and put to the torture over every paltry item on the books."

He knew how to drive a bargain with his authors when it was worth his while. One of his most striking successes in this line was with Paul Merritt, who was himself a person with a keen eye to the main chance. Harris, wishing to buy all Merritt's rights in a successful Drury Lane drama, offered him repeatedly a cheque of £8,000 for them, which he persistently refused. Determined to have his way, the tempter used to flourish it before the desired victim, with the tantalising question :

" Will you have it while you may? "

But Paul still wanted more. At last the other invited him to dinner, and at the psychological moment of the walnuts and the wine he again displayed his lure.

"Will you have it? Will you have it? Will— you—have—it? The last time of asking, 'yes' or 'no'? "

" Give it me! " shouted the scribe savagely, and snatched it from his hand.

CHAPTER XV

HUMANS AND OTHER CONTEMPORARIES

ONE knows many people, yet one is interested in but a limited number. This seems rather a truism, yet the bearings thereof are not unfruitful. Some impress you whether you like them or not. They are of all sorts; they may be people to love, people to hate—too tragic a theme for these pages —and people to respect, to tolerate, or to be unaware of, though you may be saying "How d'ye do?" to them every day. With me, for instance, Mrs. Keeley is one whose memory I cherish with delight and affection. She was always very kind to me, kind and generous, but that does not exactly account for it. The true reason, I think, is that she was so much alive. Her love of life and interest in it remained almost to the very last day of the ninety odd years of her count. Her invincible cheerfulness was a lightning cure for chills. She could rap out when she was angry—I once heard her rebuke a whole company from her box for mumbling their parts—but there was so much good nature in it that it was only the same remedy in another form. She was happy and she made you happy—that is all I know. She read the new books as they came out, she saw the plays, she lay in wait for the

Humans and Other Contemporaries

promising players as soon as their heads appeared above the horizon, and was the first to tell them, often before they knew it themselves, that what was happening to them was the promise of fame. Even when a piece was bad, she could make a reservation in favour of the player and prophesy better luck next time. Speaking for myself, I am inclined to think that liking often goes by contraries in acting as in other things. She was a comedian—well, and I was not, though I have raised a laugh with malice aforethought in my time. The saturnine Irving's chosen companion for his hours of ease was Toole, the low comedian, and mainly the cockney one at that. And, metaphorically the tragedian was at Mrs. Keeley's feet—when she was not at his, while Macready and Phelps revelled in praise of her powers. "That imp of mischief," wrote the latter . . . "about the best all-round actress I have seen."

Actors, in particular, must become select in their human interests by a sort of law of nature. Otherwise they might have to extend their sense of brotherhood to the whole "Green Room Book" for the year, with its seven or eight hundred solid pages of contemporaries, and these all boiled down —I mean the notices, of course. In a way, all the thousands it commemorates have been the comrades, known or unknown, of our professional life. And with that, what of the other arts with which one has been at least on nodding terms? Where would it all stop? I can but set down a few, a very few, of the people I have been glad to know, or sorry to have known, for it cuts both ways.

Both Sides of the Curtain

Among the former, and in a warm corner of my heart, is dear Ellen Terry. She is the most charming and kindly woman I ever met on the stage, always ready to share the limelight with others, and often adopting their suggestions at rehearsals, even when not approved by the lord of the house. Irving and I did not get on so well; it may be on my theory of affinities, because we were both in the same line of "business." I regarded him as a great character actor, but not a Shakespearean actor, except as Malvolio; but he thought very differently, though he was certainly not in the majority. Lest this should be regarded as heresy, I hasten to add that I take much the same view of Sarah Bernhardt. Though not a great character actress, she is a great melodramatic actress, with the exception of her *Phèdre*, which is, or was, really tragedy. In disposition Ellen Terry was all melting charity, and was often imposed upon through her sheer goodness of heart. It was so easy to get her cheque for any case of sorrow or distress. Her delightful book shows that she was always trying to learn, and never thought that her apprenticeship to the stage was coming to an end. It is one of the notes of the true artist; and in this respect, and only in this, she is still a child at her threescore years and ten. Irving, to do him justice, was not without a touch of the same divine dissatisfaction. He knew what it was to fail in his own esteem, and that perhaps accounted for a certain moodiness of manner in him which sometimes repelled by its suggestion of pride. He had conquered, in spite of many hindrances of nature and art, yet some of them remained to remind him, at times unpleasantly, that he was mortal.

Mary Anderson (Madame Navarro) had nothing to conquer in hindrances of this sort, and therefore she rightly relied on her natural gifts, a risk no doubt, and only to be fully justified, as this was, by the event. She made her first appearance in the United States when she was seventeen, as Juliet, and the *Louisville Journal*, a very important organ, gave her wonderful criticisms and editorial comment as well. She was a beautiful woman with a fine voice, and had temperament, though no artistic education, nor did she come of an artistic family. But it was in her to act: as a child she used to play in the garret of her home in California to the little negroes. It was her great beauty and, what is almost more essential, her charm that won her reputation. And, wisely, she did not carry the experiment too far, for she studied later on with Mr. Vanderhof. She was one of the platonic passions of William Black, the novelist—as the phrase implies, there were others as well. She left the stage after her marriage and settled at perhaps the most beautiful village in all England, Broadway in the Midlands, a dot of verdure in a glorious landscape that spreads out below you on all sides from the summit of the Worcester Beacon on the Malvern Hills. Every yard of the ground has a bit of history, for much of the life of the motherland, in arts as well as in arms, was shaped there, and Shakespeare's country is not far off. Here Langland, wellnigh six hundred years ago, wrote his great democratic poem, "The Vision of Piers the Plowman," and well within the prospect stand three mighty cathedrals, and historic battlefields by the half-dozen, Evesham, Worcester, Tewkesbury, Edgehill, Shrewsbury and Mortimer's Cross. As for little Broadway, it is a sort of settlement of souls addicted to poetry, painting and other recreations of the simple life, not unadorned with luxury and ease. Frank Millet, the American painter, passed the evening of his days there. I seemed to tremble for Madame Navarro's full enjoyment of her retreat when I heard that she had come out to play once more, and was hardly reassured to learn that it was only for war benefits and the like. My forebodings were certainly not without cause. The single day was succeeded by a week at the Coliseum, in *Pygmalion and Galatea*, for the charities of the war, and then came her representation of America in *The Pageant of Fair Women* at the Queen's Hall.

Some are greater characters off the stage, for good or ill, than they are on. They leave a name in the profession long after the public has forgotten them. Coleman, who, at the beginning of my career, had found actor-management too heavy for his shoulders, was one of these. He had a tremendous notion of the dignity of his art as embodied in himself. He acted the actor, and was still before the footlights in fancy when he took a walk or shook hands with a friend. Once, when the *Lady of Lyons* was the piece in preparation, he was duly presented by the rough-and-ready property man with the papier mâché bouquet for the heroine, which had done duty in the theatre for many years. It was yellow with frequent touchings-up of paint and varnish, and on this occasion was rather redolent of those articles and of glue. Coleman, wishing to shine before the lady who was to play Pauline, asked with stern emphasis :

" What is this? "

" It's a bookett—ain't it? " said the man.

" Faugh! fellow," said Coleman with a look of disgust, " I want fresh flowers."

" Well, you've got 'em, ain't you? " said the other. " I've touched 'em up myself. That bookett's done duty for Macready many a time, and it's been good enough for Barry Sullivan and Charles Dillon—an' they *was* actors."

There is no record of the fate of the property man. The famous Nellie Bufton, of the old Strand company, was, with extenuating circumstances, one of the same sort. She once acted a stage banquet all through in a public restaurant, refusing the mustard with a shudder of aversion, and warding off an apple tart with uplifted hands. She, however, was but probably half aware of what she was doing. The perspective is such a ticklish matter, both in the make-up and in the gestures, that these things get quite out of focus when seen too near. In Coleman's case, however, the habit had been something of a vice.

The public sometimes fall into the same error in their distorted judgments on the actor's art. They are apt to think it is all make-believe, and that the personality and the presentation are one and the same thing. The stage, as they see it, is a revel of great passions, for good or ill; therefore the stage must abound in "temptations" beyond those of the common lot. What do you think of a letter like this, now yellow with age:

"MY DEAR MISS WARD,—

"I expect you have been surprised not to hear from me before. My mother wants me to give up the idea of the stage, because she has been told it is almost impossible for a girl to get any good position unless she will consent to be immoral. Please do not mention this to my aunt. I know you would rather I told you exactly what had happened, and I have therefore written quite plainly about it."

You should have seen my answer. But no, on second thoughts, I think you shouldn't. To put it as mildly as possible, it turned on the well-known theme :

"Honour and shame from no condition rise.
Act well your part : there all the honour lies."

or otherwise, "all depends on yourself." I did not mention it to her aunt; but my fingers itched to add a postscript for the mother.

On both sides, players and public, we have to get the perspective right to understand one another. The teacher's responsibility is, perhaps, the greater of the two, because the illusions of the public are more gross. For want of this I have seen strange performances, engineered for wealthy pupils by so-called professors of stage elocution, that were a scandal to the profession. In one of these, at a

Humans and Other Contemporaries

Gaiety matinée, the débutante's chief attraction was her beautiful hair. The only thing I remember of her performance of *Romeo and Juliet* was in the scene where she drinks the potion. She suddenly threw herself forward from behind a chair and let her hair trail over her head, leaving nothing but the nape of the neck exposed, as though preparing for instant decapitation. An American admirer asked me what I thought of it. I said I thought her career might last one consecutive matinée—if the audience contrived to keep their temper. "Why," he replied, "I have just seen Mrs. B——" (a celebrated actress and wit who was in the house at the time), "and she thinks it marvellous."

"And so you think it a 'marvellous' performance?" I said, as I passed Mrs. B—— on leaving the theatre. "Well," she returned with a merry twinkle in her eye, "don't you?"

But I have met many other interesting people besides those in my own profession. A word to the would-be wise: before you declare anybody uninteresting be sure it is his fault and not yours. The very diversity of tastes has so much to do with the charm. Hamilton Aïdé, for instance, has left no great name, but what a delightful man! For years he was a valued friend of my mother and of myself, a man in society who touched all the arts, and if not necessarily to adorn them, certainly to be adorned by the contact. He wrote novels, plays, and even went so far as the "painting in water-colours," which, as we know by the famous epitaph on Lady O'Looney, is in itself a sort of passport to the celestial abodes. We spent many happy hours at his place at Ascot, where he often got up entertainments for charities and such like, at which, whenever it could possibly be done, I was most glad to help him out with a recital. He lived with a married cousin, and he was also related in that way to Mrs. Tennant, whose daughter married Stanley the explorer. The delightful dilettante of his sort is almost a vanished type, and society will be the greater sufferer by its loss.

Another of these links between society and the arts is the beautiful and charming Mrs. Alec Tweedie. As traveller, author, journalist, and above all as hostess, she has filled many parts on the stage of life and always with distinction. If I had to characterise her in a word, that word would be energy. I never knew her equal in that way. Her very books are usually schemes of travel, not mere philandering excursions for a look round. She almost discovered Mexico—went out there alone, pushed her way up to the capital, won the friendship of President Diaz and his wife, studied institutions, manners and all else that bore on the question of the "everlasting Now," and came away to write a work as solid as a treatise and readable as a novel. For the epoch of Diaz as a ruler it will always hold its place. Within a few days of the news of the Messina earthquake she had York Terrace, Regent's Park, where she then lived, simply blocked with vans crammed with clothing and other necessaries of all sorts for first aid. The terrified constables on

the beat interposed with orders to "move on,"
only to be confronted by a permit from the Chief
Commissioner. In fact, she simply annexed the
thoroughfare until the consignment was on its way
to its destination. She is actively co-operating in
the work of the Y.M.C.A. centres, a labour of
love, for it is her characteristic memorial of one of
her sons lost in the war. The other is still doing
splendid work at the Front. It is the busiest and
the most fruitfully busy life I know. Her social
relations are wide and deep. She knows everybody
and contrives to interest all in her generous schemes.
She ought long since to have had her place in one
of the Birthday Lists.

I may say that I have been rather fortunate in
all my dealings with the law. When I was but
eighteen or so, in Milan, an extortionate landlady
undertook to exploit my mother and myself, and I
went into court. Lawyers pressed forward to offer
me their services, but I said that the matter was so
simple, and the documents I had so conclusive, that
I would, like Portia, plead my own case. Which I
did, and won.

Then, in after years, came the big suits about
my rights in *Forget-me-not*, of which I have given
an account elsewhere in these pages. In England
I defied my opponents to stop me from playing the
piece, while in New York I compelled them to cease
playing it. This, although to give a certain coun-
tenance to their suit they had briefed no less a
person than Mr. Choate, afterwards American am-

bassador to England. My cause was in the hands of Mr. John H. Bird, who was not only an eminent counsel, but a fine amateur actor. He had played in *The Honeymoon* with me in Dublin, and he afterwards graced my triumph on the six hundredth performance of *Forget-me-not* in New York by taking the part of Sir Horace Welby "for this night only." There were certain things we wanted to put before the court that Mr. Bird could not put into his brief, so he instructed me to try to get them placed in the course of my cross-examination by Mr. Choate. When, therefore, the latter.put a question to me I immediately began to introduce this supplementary matter—of course not without resistance from the other side.

"Thank you, thank you, Miss Ward," said Mr. Choate, in vain trying to stop me, "that will do."

"Excuse me, but I have sworn to tell the truth, the whole truth, and nothing but the truth."

"Yes," he returned, "but not all at once."

"No," I said, "only as much as I can get in" (roars of laughter in court).

The cross-examination continued in that style, and I won my case. When it was over Mr. Choate came up and introduced himself. Strangely enough, he had never met me, although there were several ties of long standing between our families.

All this made a stir in New York—I was, in a way, so connected with the city: my grandfather had been prominent there as one of the earlier mayors.

Photo: L. Caswall Smith.

AS VOLUMNIA IN "CORIOLANUS."

Humans and Other Contemporaries

In my last experience of a lawsuit I had an unconscious victory over Sir Edward Clarke. I was called as witness in a case of Mr. Martin Harvey's, and Sir Edward was cross-examining me about the price I had paid for *Forget-me-not*, and how, since I produced it, its author had risen in value. He said:

"You know, Miss Ward, in your profession persons who receive certain emoluments for plays and acting may suddenly find themselves worth very much larger sums."

"As in yours, Sir Edward, I believe," I replied in tones that were childlike and bland.

This caused much laughter, in which the judge joined, as he leant over and remarked, "Well, I think, Sir Edward, you won't get a better answer than that!"

I really could not see where the joke came in, but it was explained to me afterwards—Sir Edward's was a notable case in point. When the laughter had subsided I said:

"Anything else, Sir Edward?"

"No, thank you!"

This was the first intimation I ever had that I was not without the comedy touch.

The authors, especially those who are that and nothing else, have, I think, a peculiar fascination for all of us. The very contrast between the far-reaching influence of their work and the comparative seclusion of their lives may account for that. You have before you most of the others on the public stage, but you may lack all personal impression of the man behind the pen—so happily called, though in derision, the quill-driver.

Charles Reade was one of the few exceptions—a terror to everybody who didn't agree with him, yet with a tender heart. I had no cause to disagree, so we got on perfectly; but what an awful spectacle it would have been if we had met in the tug of war! Niagara trying to put out Vesuvius nothing to it. When I took the Olympic in 1888, and played his *Nance Oldfield*, he presented me with a beautiful crown which had been used on the first production of the piece. It was in paste, as it was for stage use, but a thing of price at that. I gave it for sale the other day to the British Red Cross, and they were very glad to have it.

Bernard Shaw, as an exceptionality without exception, is another of the same sort. Anyhow, I must have him among my characters, though, perhaps, rather less of himself than he is willing to supply would satisfy the general demand. Like some herbs, he would give quite enough flavour by being merely rubbed round the rim of the dish. A touch is quite enough. He was once so good as to remonstrate with me for running after false gods in my choice of plays, and especially of Shakespeare. This did not prevent me from saying that if he would write a modern *Lucrezia Borgia* for me I would gladly return to the stage.

Wilkie Collins was one of those that I may class as old friends, a sort of Order of Merit more select even than the other. His one grievance in life was that his fellow-creatures would not accept him as a great creator of character, but reserved all their praise for the cunning and creepiness of his plots. His protest has found its way into his published writing. What about Count Fosco? he asks in one of his prefaces. It came often enough into his private talk.

Miss Braddon, another of my select order of the old friends, had no weakness of this sort. So far as I could see, and I saw much of her for many years, she was quite Emersonian in accepting her place in events. She might have echoed Mr. Joseph Chamberlain's "What I have said I have said," if he had been more careful to remember whom he followed in saying it. Many happy Sunday afternoons have I spent at her house at Richmond; such a nice, sweet old-fashioned house with the hospitality to match! I understand why her work was so dramatic: she had begun her life as an actress. How the arts may help one another after all, these two especially! She was happy in herself, happy in her son—only less noted in fiction than his mother, and perhaps, in the development of his powers, destined to be her equal. Where should we of the scene be without such writers to show us the way? The great authors have always been in the front rank of my favourites, and I hope some of them have returned the compliment in regard to those of my craft.

I think it was so with Longfellow; certainly he was always delightfully kind to me. He gave me a fine edition of his works signed by himself, also two little things which I prized almost above that —a pen and a lead pencil. What I like to think is that they were the two tools of his craft. Somehow his image is always connected in my mind with England, for he was more Old English in his writings than the English of our day themselves. His New England, as he saw and loved it, is the Old England of the Pilgrim Fathers preserved in lavender. The English village on its native soil has been more affected by social changes than its offspring in our land. There is a happier admixture of classes with us, less of the multi-millionaire from town in almost feudal possession, more of the sturdy and prosperous country folk. It would be harder to match his " village blacksmith," with the beautiful setting of scenery and manners, in the Old England of to-day than in the New.

Lowell, again, was a valued friend, so was Oliver Wendell Holmes. I took a young Cambridge student to see Holmes when I was visiting Boston on one of my tours, and the dear old gentleman seemed to become a boy again as he talked of college life, his youth and the like. " Now, my young friend," he said to the lad on our taking leave, " when you meet me anywhere you come up and speak to me and remind me who you are, for I never recognise young people. Life has not given any special quality to their faces."

I can sympathise with him, for I have the same difficulty and for the same reason—young people are most provokingly expressionless. In my case this embarrassment sometimes extends to the seniors;

Humans and Other Contemporaries

I have met so many thousands of fellow-creatures. People come up and speak to me, and I cannot tell whether Australia, South Africa, England or America was the scene of our first encounter, for their " Oh, Miss Ward, I'm So-and-So " is hardly a certificate of registration. In such cases, " And you'll remember me " ought not exactly to follow as a matter of course.

The American poet, Buchanan Read, was another exquisite survival of the English spirit transplanted to a happier soil. I am bound to say, however, that our meeting place was not America, but Italy, where, as a girl of fifteen, I encountered him and his wife and children at Florence. All was big about them but their proportions : they were among the tiniest people in that respect I ever saw. He also was a master of two arts, and he painted my portrait as The Bride of Abydos when Byron's creation was still at the height of her vogue.

Two years later I saw Lamartine, in his old age, in Paris. I was with my mother and Monsieur de Bois le Conte, a great friend of the poet and, like him, a man in years. He was walking in the Champs Elysées. " There, my child," said our companion, " is the great French poet ; you shall have the privilege of speaking to him." The illustrious writer was most courtly and gracious—though I hardly need say that, as he was French. I cannot tell you all the pretty speeches he made, of which my sex, my youth, and my nationality had about equal shares. A great writer he was indeed. A friend of mine never fails to read *Le Lac*, as a sort of annual service, to keep him, as he puts it, "in tune with the Infinite." I don't wonder at that: with Gray's "Elegy," it is still another "Psalm of Life," solving no mystery indeed, but at least posing it in its terms of love and longing with the most exquisite felicity.

The giant past of his generation was the Napoleonic epoch. I need not say what our giant present is to-day. That earlier time still lived in many hale and hearty survivals: when I was eight the Battle of Waterloo itself was only thirty years old. I easily came to know Isabey, miniature painter to the first Napoleon, who took a great interest in my mother's work in that line, and never spared encouragement and advice. A quaint little dried-up figure in black silk stockings and trunks. With him was often Count de Waldeck, another contemporary painter, who lived long enough to enable me to meet him in 1873—when I came over after the siege of Paris by the Germans—nigh sixty years after Waterloo. He was then one hundred and eight years old, bright, breezy, alert, and quite busy with a new scheme of education by the eye. All I remember of it was that it kept him hard at work painting slides on glass for schools. Death claimed him not long after, and, I fear, made off with the scheme as well as its author. I was going to play Wills's *Sappho* at the time, and he sketched a little figure of the heroine for me and wrote a few lines of one of her poems from memory. When we verified these at the Biliothèque Nationale we found them all but literally correct. What was the secret,

Humans and Other Contemporaries

I wonder? "Never say die," I suppose, for perhaps that was said for him at the last, or Death himself waived the confession of defeat.

Bouguereau was painting for all he was worth at that time, and he was worth a good deal in pounds, shillings and pence if you reckon it in that way. He turned out saints *à la Raffaelle* and peasant girls with equal facility—the latter by preference, so far as I was concerned, as they were nearer to life. I remarked to him once, after looking at a study of a peasant girl just stepping into the river to bathe, that the figure seemed too thin and skimpy for the part, whereas in his other works, in which the rustic types appeared clothed and in their right mind, they had all the fullness and bloom of youth. His explanation was: "I cannot get the country folk to sit to me for the nude, and so have to depend on the stock models of the studio and of city life."

As one star rises, you will generally find another ready to fade. This was his experience. He lived and worked to the dawn of a new and totally different school, represented by Sargent, just beginning to get into his stride with a bold impressionism, in which everything was indicated rather than carried out in detail, and the essentials of light and movement and the sense of values were the all in all. Adieu to the celestial hierarchy with their impeccable toilettes of cloud, or stuffs fresh from the loom, and place for the men and women of the day in their costumes as they lived, and with their grace and distinction which seemed to show the earth in rivalry with the skies. Then, not without his pathetic warning to the younger man, they passed on their divergent ways.

So much for my human contemporaries; a word as to the others—I mean my dogs. I am afraid I have already mentioned some of them, but do what I may I can't keep them out whenever there is a chance of getting them in. They are so *unfailing;* your affections are always on safe ground.

I had three in forty years: Mouche, who lived ten years, Thekla fourteen, and Marianto sixteen— all good ages, and for the simple reason that I never allowed them to grow fat. I named them after the characters I was playing when they came into my life. Thekla was after Thekla von Thurenau, in Wingfield's play *Despite the World*, Marianto after Maria Antonia, Duchessa Padovani—which I played at the Avenue Theatre with George Alexander in his production of *The Struggle for Life*. All have been ladies. Gyp, their present successor, is the first gentleman. Female dogs are much more affectionate, male ones more selfish. I think one sex as intelligent as the other. Marianto, a small Manchester terrier, had the most affectionate disposition and a fondness for petting which exceeded anything I have ever known. I am sorry I only made a duchess of her; she ought to have been a princess. She would remain in almost any position for an indefinite time, so long as she found herself in contact with me, and she had a wonderful comprehension of anything that was repeated to her a few times. At one time she manifested a great interest in the proceedings below stairs, and would steal down to the kitchen on every opportunity. I cured her entirely of this propensity by talking to her at the head of the stairs, and indicating with a gesture that the place below was taboo for her. I pointed out that it was not the proper thing for a lady to haunt the kitchen, that her place was above stairs, and she at once abandoned the practice. We had a little comedy every morning in my room. She used to come to me immediately my maid rose, and remain on the bed till my breakfast was brought without showing the slightest inclination to share it. After a while I would offer her a piece of bread and butter, of which, when there was nothing in competition with it, she was fond. But she would look at it and turn her head away, as though saying, "No, thank you; there's metal more attractive on the tray. If you can't spare a bit of that, let matters remain as they are." I repeated the offer, with the same result. I coaxed—no response; her head was turned every way but towards the plainer fare. Then I said, "Oh, very well, you don't want it. Here, Khalifa" —this to a beautiful blue Persian cat—"Khalifa!" That always settled it; her mind changed at once, and her coyness and the bread and butter disappeared together.

Then, although I said something about Thekla in Australia, and how I got her through quarantine by just putting my foot down, I quite forgot to mention the sulky purser who was the cause of all my trouble. On the voyage to Melbourne poor Thekla managed somehow to incur his dislike; if

Both Sides of the Curtain

you had known her you would have known whose
fault it must have been. We joined the ship at
Ceylon, and two state-rooms had been reserved, by
arrangement with the company, for our accommodation at Colombo. There was a great demand for
rooms on board; the reserved rooms for us in some
way appeared to disturb the purser's equanimity—
at any rate, the courtesy usually shown by officials
in his position was very distinctly wanting. As we
neared Australia hints were frequently dropped that
under the quarantine laws then in force my pet
would not be allowed to land with me, and my affection for the little creature being well known, and
the purser's dislike equally clear, the matter became
subject of much talk and sympathy among all the
passengers whose hearts were in the right place.
Here, then, our drama had reached its second act;
the antagonists in presence, the cause of quarrel
posed. I was not idle, you may be sure. On reaching Albany I telegraphed my managers a pressing request that they would interest themselves with the
authorities to obtain the necessary permission for
Thekla's entry into the colony. The purser, on the
other hand, made no secret of his determination to
keep us apart, and his face began to light up with
a smile of anticipated triumph that was odious to
see. When we got in I made no attempt to leave;
and in a short time we saw the managers board the
ship with the official vet, who, after a brief examination of Thekla, announced that she might land at
once—her quarantine being her owner's arms.
Curtain : Thekla trotting gaily along the quay behind

266

her smiling mistress; villain of the piece bursting with disgust and discomfiture in the background.

Gyp, a little black and tan terrier, is simply the dearest—but there, I somehow feel that everybody ought to know that. He goes through exactly the same performance as Marianto, and with exactly the same result when I threaten to call the cat. There's intelligence for you. He has quaint little ways of his own; he never meets or greets different people in the same fashion, and he never forgets his human friends, though he may not see them for months. He never mistakes one for another, but takes up the acquaintance where he left off at the last meeting. When I come home from the theatre at night he meets me with a joyous bark at the front door, rushing down from the top of the house to get to the door before me.

CHAPTER XVI

BY THE BOUDOIR FIRE

THERE are worse places than the boudoir fire for retirement and reflection on a busy life, especially when the glow is tempered by an occasional return to the draughts of the stage. The suitable domestic properties are at hand in the spoils of travel, in curios, in heirlooms—in pictures, the brother's desk and chair and pen, one's own tools of the dressing-table and what not, each with its history of a birthday or other jollification. Then perhaps a turn in the drawing-room where the burglars once got in, and couldn't get out again farther than a couple of gardens off before they were nabbed. What does all this mean, but that one's own little home is one's own little home, and there's an end on't?

What do I think of it all? Well, upon my word, I really don't quite know. I think I have had a right royal time, but that will hardly do. What may the reader expect on such a solemn occasion? Something improving, no doubt. Let me see, then, the drama as the true linker-up of nations and of races throughout the world. This ought to do for a paradox that may at least make him sit up. What about literature? it will be said. Oh, it makes a good second; I will concede no more. The languages keep it hopelessly pigeon-holed into parts, for translations, at best, are but poor substitutes for the live nerve of the idiom. The foreign play, if it is to win its way, is no translation at all, but a transfusion of blood—a very different thing. When that is done, and well done, you are as acceptable in China as in Peru. It speaks in terms of action and of life, and the players use the real words of a universal language of the passions and of the heart.

That world tour of mine, with a budget of good plays, what a first-rate course of education it was for the tourist as well as the toured. People of all colours, customs, modes of talking and thinking too, I dare say, yet all alike under the common spell of feeling. It's really a more than Imperial bond of union in its way, as something touching the brotherhood of man. But, if you don't take care, the very bigness of the survey sometimes makes your own play look quite provincial to yourself, like something in manners and customs that has happened all in a corner. 'Ware there, or it would mean ruin! You have to keep constantly saying, " No, this is quite all right, *the* thing in all that's worth being and doing, and those who don't think so had better key up to it at once." Another curious thing, though a minor one, is that in some places the mere dressing of a modern piece is quite a lesson in " the fashions " for the audience. You see signs of it as you take your walks abroad. The local Penelope, perhaps, has been too manifestly up all night stitching and unstitching to keep herself in the movement

for the *mode*, and here again you have at least a
sisterhood to match the other I was talking of just
now. The fashions make good Puck's boast of gird-
ling the planet; and here or there, a furtive touch
to head, hand or foot shows the wildest under the
spell. I quite agree with what was once said about
that: the picturesque races are quite tired of being
a show for the traveller. They want to dwell in his
memory as Paris abroad, not as Honolulu at home.
The very nigger is a *boulevardier* in his own conceit.
When the women come into power they'll work on
that—you see! The flag's all right in its way, but
the skirt, too, is a power. It is a dreadful drop for
the artist in his sense of the dignity of his calling
and of his appeal on the higher plane of the heart
and the mind, but it is none the less a fact. The
more intelligent races are the weakest in this way
because of their sense of form. A travelled Bengalee
is tailor-made from top to toe, and more than a match
for his conqueror, not only in the niceties of the
Bhavagad, but in socks and ties.

When I am quite comfortable by my boudoir fire
I sometimes amuse myself by reckoning how I have
worked and how many miles I have trotted about
this planet. Of course, I don't pretend to include
daily walks and excursions to buy a *fichu*, but only
journeys on the regular business of my profession.
The trip round the world, for instance—the special
one so named in the record—ran to 35,533 miles—
not as the crow flies, naturally, for the ridiculous
creature appears simply to follow his own nose in
the promptings of a vacuous mind. No, I mean

the to and from work between the scores of local centres and their circumferences. Add to this, again, the sixteen crossings of the Atlantic, without saying a word about the tours of the British Isles, etc., and you have 48,000 more, or a grand total of about 85,000 miles all on business.

Now, then, for the work done. Well, from first to last, as I make it, in drama alone, without saying a word about the operas mentioned elsewhere, I have played in seventy-seven pieces, great and small, and by a large proportion mainly the former. Shakespeare was a large contributor, and the rest were important ventures in ancient or modern work. I am not boasting about it in the least; many of my comrades have done as much, some have done more —I once had a scoring match of this kind with Mr. W. H. Vernon, and he soon passed me on the way to the winning-post. But, taking it just for what it is and no more, what thousands of lines of parts learned letter perfect, and, once more, nearly all of it literature. Why, the whole profession ought to be able to talk like a book in the choicest of phrase, and to set an example even in the way of saying "pass the salt." As for sensations and situations, we have sampled them all, from a courtship to a deed of blood, in which perhaps we have the widest range.

No wonder the actors are sometimes tempted to lose sight of the distinction between themselves and the characters they play. They are kings and queens in a way, and the incense they breathe exceeds in pungency anything offered to the most popular rulers of the world. But, like kings, they have to learn the limits of their power, or woe betide. They have now to dominate their liegemen, now to humour and to coax. If they fail in the last they may never get to Madame Tussaud's. The old actors seemed to have cringed overmuch, to judge by their prologues, though Cook could tell a Liverpool audience that every stone in their city was cemented by the blood of a negro. But it was Dutch courage, no doubt, in his case, and he must have felt badly about it, as my countrymen say, when the fumes had passed off. Ellen Terry tells us how "Henry" once lost his temper on the failure of a piece, and showed it, but he seems never to have repeated the experiment. Note how he at once gave way afterwards on the subject of booked seats for the pit. In his day, in short, we had to rule by constitutional methods and to learn how to yield with grace. But we had our reward. It was a great epoch for us, perhaps as great as any in theatrical annals. We were admired, honoured, respected—aye, there's the rub. The palmy days of the stage did not end with the dynasties of the Kembles. The Victorian was a great age in that as in all else. Choose your subject for "tragedy, comedy, history, pastoral, pastoral-comical, historical-pastoral," and all the rest of it in its most shining examples, and beat it if you can.

What a pity we have no more abiding means of comparison! You can compare this painter with that in present and past, this writer in the same way —not a single link in the evidence is wanting. It is notoriously harder in the case of the orators, but

AS THE DUCHESS IN "THE ARISTOCRAT."

there are the speeches, for what they are worth. The players leave no trace. No wonder they are so insistent on payment on delivery, both in praise and pence. Who can tell exactly how the exquisite Bracegirdle managed that, "Oh, my dear, dear bud," that turned the heads of players and public alike; who reconstitute a scene of Jordan or of Faucit? Stay, in the last case somebody can—your humble servant. I once heard her, years after her formal retirement, at a charity performance or something of the sort. In this case, what a disappointment! All elocution, no life, soul, or spirit. She seemed to have been drilled into it by the ghost of Walker's Dictionary, and to have never for one single moment come into full and free possession of her text or of herself. It was like a good little girl reciting a lesson, so that the very gesture seemed superfluous, for the hands should have been behind her back. And yet this electrified our fathers, and sent them pensive and edified to bed.

The "march of improvement" may come to our aid in course of time. The films have given us movement already, the 'phones have given us speech, something else may give us "atmosphere," and there you are. Here and there, at this very day, you may have bottled orations to order; and further mechanical discoveries may suit the action to the word, the word to the action, until the effect, in its rounded completeness, stands out in every attribute of life. Then we may look for a Westminster Abbey of the resuscitated past, and be able to call spirits from the vasty deep by simply unlocking the door

of a cabinet. Already the virtuoso or the valetudin-
arian may ring up his opera or play after a fashion
without stirring from his fireside. Drop a shilling
in the slot and lo behold! you are at Covent Garden,
or what was once Drury Lane. I admit it too often
seems to come from the bowels of the earth, as from
gnomes in torture, but wait and see.

The drama will change—that you can safely say
—but in what direction? Ah! Perhaps in that of
less demand for action, action, action, especially on
the English stage. Even now we have something of
the kind in France, where they were able to find
room for Dumas the Younger, as well as for Scribe
and Sardou. Coquelin's dissipated little duke in the
Dumas piece talked daggers of infamy to his wife,
but used none. I really forget if he was run through
the body in a duel at the end; it would have been
a mistake. The British public never has had much
patience with mere dramatic conversation. The
famous philosophic disquisition on the theory of the
vibrion in the Dumas play would bore us to extinc-
tion, but to quote the mendicant in the story,
though "your 'eart's uncommon stony, there's
'opes for you yet." Shaw has come to town. Some
of the literary plays, like Stevenson's, or those of
Henry James, make beautiful reading; and if audiences could be convened by selection might serve
for everything but a run. As it was, poor James,
especially, used to sit in torture behind the curtains
of his box, registering every hiss on his heart strings,
and when it was over finding no relief but tears as
he rushed from the house, while gallery and pit,

with their thumbs down, were roaring, "Author! Author!" for the final sacrifice.

The late Smith-Dorrien controversy, I think, seems to point the way to some sort of change. The General is no carpet knight, for he helped to save them at Mons by holding up a whole German army with a handful of men, until they found cover again under the shelter of their guns. He was allowed, therefore, to point a moral, without incurring the penalty with a sneer. He appealed to music-hall managers to give us a little more variety on the variety stage. Why, he said, rely so much on "exhibitions of scantily dressed girls and songs of doubtful character?" This especially in the interest of our soldiers and sailors, who, he felt sure, would be better pleased by the change. The spirit of the nation, as represented by these heroes, was worthy of better treatment. It was not so much the mere impropriety of these appeals as their incredible vulgarity. He could enjoy his Harry Lauder with anyone, but the other man, out for a laugh at any cost, evidently brought the deepest dejection to his soul. The managers joined issue at once. Some agreed and pleaded "not guilty"; others said the public was the true arbiter, and while it continued to give you crowded houses what on earth were you to do? The judicious, who were not in management, joined in the fray. Mr. Poel deplored the brisk demand for "burglar plays, playlets, and sketches"; and he, or another, quoted the advertisement from a theatrical weekly paper: "Geoffrey Rivers climbs up the waterspout of the house of his friend in Pont Street in order to make love to that friend's beautiful better half."

There is no doubt of it, some of our films would bring a visible blush to the face of a negro. In one of my trips round America the fare at the hotel was so atrocious that the coloured man, in serving it, used always to turn his head away. I asked the cause: "Missee, I 'shamed to offer you de food." It was all he could do in the circumstances, but with the help of some of our films I fancy he would have achieved the blush.

The Board of Film Censors, organised by the more respectable firms in the trade, have done their best, and now perhaps their only danger lies in going too far. For, as things stand, the sauce for the goose of the music-halls will soon be the sauce for the gander of the theatres, since the two are merging into one, and the Lord Chamberlain will be more powerful than ever. Among their grounds of rejection are: " Exceedingly passionate love scenes "—the late Mrs. Bernard Beere used to revel in one on which the scandalised curtain seemed ready to fall of its own accord; " Antagonistic relations of capital and labour "—in one case, far enough back to be quite under the old dispensation, an excellent dramatisation of Disraeli's *The Two Nations* was refused on this very ground; "Scenes depicting the realistic horrors of warfare "—if we had more of these perhaps there would be fewer submarines on the prowl.

Only think of the innings for the cranks!

By the Boudoir Fire

It might come to mean a return to the Puritan severities of the Commonwealth.

George Russell has given us an amusing account of a case before the licensing magistrates, which was only saved to common sense by the cleverness of the cross-examining counsel. The lady in the case, a hostile witness against the applicants for the license, told the committee that the performance on a certain evening had been "far, far worse than anything she had ever seen."

"We must know your standard of comparison," said counsel for the applicant. "What have you seen? Have you ever seen a ballet?"

"Oh, never, never!"

"Have you ever seen a pantomime?"

"Never."

"Have you ever seen any theatrical performance of any kind?"

"Yes; I once saw a play acted at a temperance fête at the Victoria Coffee Palace."

"Sir," said counsel, turning to the chairman with a rosy smile, "on behalf of my client I must submit that the witness's experience is inadequate for purposes of comparison."

It called to mind what Sydney Smith had written years before that:

"These people not only stay away from the comedies of Congreve and Farquhar, for which they may easily enough be forgiven; but they never go to see Mrs. Siddons in *The Gamester* or in *Jane Shore*. The finest exhibition of talent and the most beautiful moral lessons are interdicted if displayed at the theatre. There is something in the word 'play-house' which seems so closely connected in their minds with sin and Satan, that it stands in their vocabulary for every species of abomination."

As all this affects the stage censorship, it lies entirely in the hands of the stage itself. It must steadily set its face against indecency in the guise of art. As Gilbert, the first of comic writers, found you could be funny without pruriency, so the Tragic Muse may make the same discovery for herself. The growing taste for the swear word, of which Shaw set the example, may lead us and him anywhere but where we want to go. A dull fellow at a loss for emphasis may easily hit on blasphemy as his next happy thought. Other dull fellows will think they have only to go one more on him, and then where shall we be? In the gutter, of a certainty. But what about my own swear words in *The Basker* and in *The Aristocrat*? Evil communications corrupt good manners, that's all.

The master of them all is not free from reproach. As I have already said elsewhere, his *Ghosts* was one of the plays in which I absolutely refused to appear. Somewhere in his published writings he records the anxiety with which he watched the results of the first performance in Norway. Would his own countrymen rise to it, or would they not? They sank to it, at any rate, and he came away with a sense of triumph. Yet what was it, after all, but the triumph of another fat boy in "Pickwick" out to make your flesh creep at all costs?

After centuries of steady work on the purification of manners we have all come to the conclusion that there are certain things we know, but don't want to hear about, in the actual cautery of stage dialogue or public discussion of any sort. The more strictly we adhere to this reserve the more surely can we get any effect we want within the limits of decency imposed by the conventions—if you choose to call them so—of the tastes of the age. The raw material of bygone manners will no longer do the business: it must be treated, for any profitable use, as crude pitch or cod liver is treated for the toilet or the sick room. The emulsion serves.

I have always regretted that I missed Paris during the war of 1870 as a besieged resident. The work in the ambulances would have been a lesson in pure self-forgetfulness hardly to be had in any other way. I was in America at the time, and there was no possibility of return before the gates were closed; moreover, I had my ailing father in my charge. It was the first crisis in our time of the fate of France, and the duty would have found me in the flower of my age and energies.

The present crisis of the same kind finds me not young, and not exactly a female Hercules, so what can I do but knit socks and breathe wishes for the four lands I love the best—my own, its dear motherland, and after these, but still in touch with them, Italy and France?

My mother and my brother Albert were in Paris from the beginning of the siege, and they saw it through. We kept in touch with each other as best we could. Here is one of our little cards from

Both Sides of the Curtain

Albert, dated " Paris, Jan. 27, 1871," and marked
" No. 75." It reads :

" BELOVED ONES,

" Mother and self quite well. No shells have yet
reached our domicile, and not likely to.

" Your loving son and brother,

" AL."

It was sent out by balloon, and it reached me
Feb. 17.

My mother took a prominent part in a begging
march in support of an ambulance which realised
fifteen thousand francs. Soon after the Germans
had completed the investment hams were selling at
two hundred francs, and everything else in proportion. Everybody was rationed on the card system,
and her servant had usually to wait some six hours
for their allowance. At last, all she brought back
in the way of food was a piece of horsemeat, three
inches square, for all three of them. Now and then
came treats. Here are some of my mother's jot-
tings, written when it was all over :

" Doctor Gordon had come running eagerly up
the stairs with a present for me. Some friend had
given him and his coadjutor, Sir James Innes, M.D.,
two ordinary smoked herring. They had kept one
for themselves, and here was Doctor Gordon with
the other one.

* * * * *

" During the armistice Doctor Gordon got hold
of a piece of white bread-and-butter and gave it to

me. The butter I ate as if it had been an apple, being quite out of carbon of my own at the time.

*   *   *   *   *

"During the armistice Colonel Stuart Wortley gave me several hundred bonds for food he brought over, for me to distribute among the poor.

*   *   *   *   *

"Albert ate the meat of the horse, mule, donkey, kangaroo and elephant. The elephant was pink, like the inside of a conch shell, and the flesh of the finest fibre, and both he and Doctor Gordon found it excellent. Dogs were two prices: Newfoundlands six francs a pound and small dogs three francs. Two rats ran into our apartment. The concierge came and killed them and begged them of us for food. Rats were then selling for two francs apiece. Yet some people have asserted there was plenty of food.

*   *   *   *   *

"The Marquis de Jouffroy executed one of the most difficult feats of the war. He knew every tree and rock between Paris and Versailles, where his aunt lived. He slipped out of Paris unseen and reached Versailles on foot, took a bushel basket, filled it with white bread, butter and chickens, and crept back into Paris, with this heavy basket on his shoulder, unmolested and unhurt. His escape, for the Germans threw an electric light all the time around Paris, is a marvel to himself and to his friends to this day. The contents of his basket he divided between his aunt, the Countess D——, and me."

Both Sides of the Curtain

Honest soul! He at least ends on a strong note, and where there is fire there is warmth.

Yet there is one serious appreciation on which I must say a final word. They were all, oh so nice to me on my eightieth birthday—on the stage with a meeting all to ourselves at the St. James's Theatre and a charmingly illuminated address, and off the stage with all sorts of tributes of esteem and affection. Sir George Alexander was good enough to say that I first taught him the value of Courage. I had forgotten the service, but I cannot part with the compliment—from such a quarter who could? And I venture to add a rider in this form:

"Yes, Courage, but not for yourself, nor even for your profession alone, but for your race. National Service is the mighty drama in which woman, as well as man, is now taking one of the star parts, and by sheer faculty of brain and hand winning emancipation without a charter or a blow. So please consider this little message addressed to the Whole Community, by

"GENEVIÈVE WARD."

INDEX

285

Index

Index

Index

Index

Index

Index

Index

CPSIA information can be obtained at www.ICGtesting.com
Printed in the USA
LVOW032145220712

291074LV00010B/62/P